THE NEW
CAPTURED HARVEST

THE NEW CAPTURED HARVEST

Creative Crafts from Nature

TERENCE MOORE

PHOTOGRAPHS BY MICHELLE GARRETT

READ ON
PUBLICATIONS
INCORPORATED

TORONTO • EDMONTON • VANCOUVER
SAN FRANCISCO

JUST FOR SUZY

This edition published in 1996 by
READ ON
Publications Inc.,
100 The East Mall, Unit 5,
Toronto, Ontario M8Z 5X2, Canada
Phone (416) 503-3444
Fax (416) 503-9386

Produced by
Anness Publishing Limited
1 Boundary Row
London SE1 8HP

Publisher: Joanna Lorenz
Project Editor: Joanne Rippin
Designer: Lisa Tai

Typeset by MC Typeset Ltd, Rochester, Kent, UK

Printed and bound in Hong Kong

Contents

INTRODUCTION

In this book, I have designed a new range of unusual displays that, I hope, are a little more exciting than the standard dried-flower display work, which are often seen only as a collection of grasses and straw flowers. There is now a far wider choice of high-quality materials available from good suppliers and, of course, much can be collected from gardens and the countryside, especially in autumn, when nature provides a carpet of material, giving the enthusiastic arranger a chance to create some stunningly colourful displays.

Most of the materials used in this book are my personal favourites and they include many non-floral items, such as mushrooms, cones, nuts, dried oranges and pomegranates and preserved leaves. By using a combination of materials collected from country walks and the garden and a few bought items, a large range of designs can be made fairly inexpensively; this is in stark contrast to shop-bought arrangements, where, naturally, the price is fairly high because the skill and time required to make the piece must be paid for.

This book contains a range of designs for different locations, using both all dried and a combination of dried and fresh material. If you are new to arranging, there are plenty of smaller projects to start with which will give you a good range of skills, so that you can move on to more complex projects. If you are an old hand at arranging, I hope that you will find all the projects both demanding and enjoyable.

Remember that the material listing is only a guide: if you have trouble obtaining a particular item, or wish to create the piece in a different colour combination, substitute something else. Don't be afraid to experiment: you will soon be able to design and create individual pieces that ideally fit the space you require them for.

Spend plenty of time mastering the basic skills described in the Techniques section and refer back to them whenever they are mentioned at the beginning of a project. Before starting a project read through all the notes thoroughly and make sure that you have the required list of materials and tools. Prepare plenty of space to work in and give yourself plenty of time. As you work through the project, remove all waste material from the work area, so you can see the display clearly as it progresses. Stand back frequently from your work, viewing it from different angles to see if the shape and mix are correct. Think about the visual relationships between the materials you are adding – colour, shape, height, texture – it's easy to keep adding items enthusiastically, losing control of the overall plan.

If possible, try to complete the project without stopping; it is often hard to go back to a piece without changing course slightly, or forgetting a half-learnt skill.

Save all the delicate items, such as roses and peonies, until the very last so that the risk of damage to them is reduced. This is particularly important for shop-purchased items as they will have been quite expensive to buy.

I hope that you enjoy creating these projects as much as I have enjoyed designing and making them: above all, I hope that they will give you confidence to create a wealth of your own designs that will provide continuing pleasure.

TERENCE MOORE

Left: *Autumn Fabric and Flower Swag*
(see page 84)

Right: *top; Fireplace Variation (see page 68)*
middle; Napkin Rings (see page 80)
bottom; Spring Candle Ring (see page 36)

TECHNIQUES

FOAM-FILLED FLOWERPOTS

Flowerpots of all shapes and sizes make extremely good containers for a vast range of different dried materials. Old terracotta lends itself to this use perfectly, especially when the design combines a cream, church-style candle. Don't be afraid to use terracotta for all types of displays and for different occasions: even at a formal dinner party, where fine furniture is used, the rustic charm of terracotta makes a stunning contrast with polished wood, especially when plenty of dark green moss is combined with the displays. Of course, it's important that a polished surface is well protected from the rough base of a terracotta pot. If the table display is for a particular occasion and fairly temporary, plastic sheeting can be cut to

size and used as a protective base. This is particularly good if you dress the area around the pots with moss to hide the sheeting. For a more permanent display, you can glue a piece of felt to the base of the pot, or use self-adhesive pads.

Pots can also be painted with a water-based stain or paint, to match the chosen location. Dark wood-stains look particularly good when applied to smooth new terracotta. Apply the stain fairly generously, changing the brush direction all the time; this will create a wood-finish effect. Remember to paint the rim of the pot and the first 2.5 cm (1 in) or so inside the pot; you will then have an attractive finish to the edge of the pot, if it is simply going to be used for moss and a candle. It will also be suitable for

any small display, where the edge of the pot will show.

If old pots are hard to find, choose new pots with care: many are fairly unattractive. Wherever possible, use hand-thrown pots. Left outside in the garden for a few months, pots will develop an attractive covering of lichens, algae and salts. Before working with a pot you have left outside, though, bring it into a warm place to dry out completely. Terracotta holds vast amounts of water in its porous structure, just waiting to leave a ring on your favourite polished table.

Terracotta also works very well outside, combined with a large range of different materials. It is particularly attractive used on the patio table with the food and wine, especially on a summer evening with a few

Left: Old terracotta makes a wonderful container for all types of floral arrangements. If you are lucky enough to own a hoard of pots, make good use of them. Even a collection arranged on the kitchen window sill, combined with a few sprigs of dried herbs will produce an attractive display.

candle pots and plenty of green moss. Of course, there are many other types of china, porcelain and clay pots that can be used, so that the finished display matches its surroundings. Even plain glass containers make good bases for display work, although the preparation is a little different. When using clear glass, the foam needs to be cut smaller than the inside area of the container and the space between the foam and the sides filled with moss or pot pourri to hide the foam. When using fine china or glass, take great care not to force the foam into place, just in case the strain is too much and the container breaks. Always work on a non-slip surface; even a thin, damp sponge under the container will ensure that the base does not slide around on your work bench or kitchen table.

YOU WILL NEED:

Materials:
florist's dry foam
  block
terracotta flowerpot
hay or sphagnum
  moss

Tools:
knife
glue gun (optional)

1 Hold the foam block near the pot and trim it to roughly the same shape as the pot. Be cautious and cut small pieces off gradually, leaving the foam block a little larger than the inside diameter of the pot.

2 Push the trimmed foam firmly into the pot so that it goes right to the bottom. You may find that the foam is a little large. Now is the time carefully to trim some more foam, until you have a perfect fit.

3 Pack the spaces around the foam with hay or moss, pushing it down firmly so that the foam is held in place. For a really permanent fit, put a little glue on to the pot and the foam. This will ensure that the foam will not come out.

4 Trim the foam to the required height. This finished height will depend on the design you are making. You may need to trim the foam so that it is level with the top of the pot; when doing this, use the rim of the pot as the guide for the knife, having first trimmed away any loose packing hay or moss.

FOAM-FILLED BASKETS

Baskets offer the widest choice of containers for floral work. Although imported from around the world, many baskets are very cheap. When choosing a basket, check that it stands evenly on a flat surface. If it does not, it is sometimes possible to trim a piece away without damage to the base, but do this with care, making sure that no sharp edges are left to damage the surface underneath, and, of course, never trim so much away that the basket collapses. If your basket is the right colour and size, but the shape is uneven, the trimmed foam will often correct the shape, but the foam will need to be a tight fit.

Choose a basket that suits the style of the finished display: heavy, chunky baskets are best for dark winter colours and perfect to use with nuts, cones and other woody items. The lighter weaves are perfect for spring and summer displays, especially when they are to be placed on a fabric-draped table. If the weave is fairly open, pack the area around the foam with moss so that the foam cannot be seen.

Old or antique baskets make more unusual containers, but often need to be used with more care, because the materials will have dried out and may be brittle. It is possible to change the appearance of a tatty or cheap basket completely, either by spraying it with florist's paint or covering it with moss, hay or a combination.

Throughout this book, you will find designs using baskets, and a few basic rules are common to all of them. Make sure that the foam is firmly fitted in the basket; if you have trimmed it too small, pack the area

around the foam with hay or moss, so that there is no risk of the finished display falling out. Never be afraid to use a basket that has a handle. If you feel your design doesn't need the handle, a strong pair of cutters will remove it from most baskets.

YOU WILL NEED:

Materials: **Tools:**
florist's dry foam   knife
basket   pliers
stub (floral) wire

1 Place the block of dry foam next to the basket and trim it to roughly the same shape. If the basket is large, or of an unusual shape, you may need more than one block of foam.

2 Push the trimmed foam into the basket. If it is a little over-sized, remove it and trim a little more foam away. Try to keep the foam on the large side, so that it is a tight fit. Depending on the shape and size of the basket, you may need to trim foam away around the top of the basket. Remember, many basket displays are trimmed around the edge with moss, so the foam needs to be as close a fit to the basket as possible, so that there are plenty of fixing points.

3 Push a stub (floral) wire through the side of the basket and across the top of the foam, twisting the ends back around the tightened wire, *this will ensure that the foam will not fall out of the basket. If the foam is a really tight fit, this isn't necessary.*

COPPER GARLAND RING

Copper rings are a strong and inexpensive way of creating a good base for many different types of design, most commonly, garlands. They are available in a large range of sizes from around 30 cm (12 in) diameter to 60 cm (24 in). Rings are covered in moss or hay, which makes a good, firm base for other materials. Be careful not to add too much moss or hay, however, because this increases the surface area to be covered. In the book, you will find designs for chandeliers, candlerings, all using a copper ring as the base. Although the basic method for covering the ring is the same, do take note of the minor variations in each project.

You will need a fair amount of materials to cover even the smallest ring. As a very general rule, for a 30–35 cm (12–14 in) ring, 6–8 bunches of material are needed to give a good covering. When all the bunches have been trimmed to size and the waste disposed of, divide them into four equal piles and use one pile for each quarter of the ring. This will soon show if you have enough to finish the project, and re-making a quarter of the ring is far less trouble than getting three-quarters of the way round and then discovering that you have used the last item.

When fixing the material with reel wire, a few basic rules apply and you need to keep them in mind at all times, although variations are explained in each project. Some of these also apply to making swags.

You will need:

Materials:
reel of florist's wire
copper ring
sphagnum moss

Tools:
cutters

Tie the reel of wire to one of the copper wires of the ring to make a firm starting point. Then take a good handful of moss and hold it on to both the top and the bottom of the copper ring, to form an even layer of moss. Wrap the wire around the ring, fixing the moss in place. Repeat this process all the way round the ring until it is evenly covered.

TIPS FOR ATTACHING MATERIALS WITH REEL WIRE

- Always prepare the materials first, cutting away the waste from the stems and making separate, neat piles of each item.
- Practise laying items on the ring without tying them in place, to give a general idea of how the combination works.
- Add the materials to the ring, so that there are no gaps along the inside and outside edge. It is very easy to keep adding material along the top edge of the ring when standing above it, and to forget the other edges.
- Add the materials in a zig-zag fashion across the ring, remembering to use all the different varieties.
- Always fix the materials at the base of the stems and never at the flower heads. Tying too high up the stems produces a very flat-looking display; you should always be able to push your fingers between the material and the ring.
- Frequently hang the part-finished work on a wall, and stand back to make sure the materials are evenly balanced and well spaced.

TOPIARY BASE

Topiary often appears to be a rather daunting task, with a number of different elements to consider. Before the start of a topiary project, it is well worth reading all the various steps and being quite clear on the direction required to achieve a good result. This area of design requires – even more than most of these projects – a real feel for proper sense of balance and shape.

Choose the container carefully, since this will dictate the finished shape and size of the piece. As a very general rule, the floral element, i.e., the ball of flowers or chosen material, will need to be about a third larger in diameter than the diameter of the top of the container. Of the total height of the finished display, the container, the trunk and the floral sphere will each need to be a third. These are general rules, however, and are often broken to solve a particular problem. It is also a matter of personal taste; your preference may be to have a very short trunk with a large floral sphere and a large container. The important rule to remember is to plan your chosen route first. This discipline is particularly important when making a pair of trees; there is simply no room for a hit-and-miss approach here, because only a good balance will make the project work. Make both at the same time, and select identical materials, if possible. Lastly, select tree trunks that are on the thick side; these always give a better balance to the finished piece.

When using large or precious pots as the base for the topiary display, first set the trunk into a plastic pot that you can then put inside your good-quality pot without any fear of breakage. This also has the advantage that the display can easily be removed to another container.

The base for the floral part of the work need not be a foam sphere: a chicken wire and moss ball can be fixed to the top of the trunk with a staple gun.

Topiary work requires really neat, well wired bunches of materials, because a great deal of material will be pushed into a fairly small surface area of foam. Untidy wiring can be the main cause of a failed project, because the stems will not push neatly into the base.

When working with just one type of material always add bunches one next to another; never work into the middle of spaces, because this just creates smaller and smaller spaces to fill. When working with a number of different materials, add around

Left: *Using just one variety of material for a topiary tree not only produces a stunning arrangement, but is much easier to create than a tree with a collection of different bunches.*

8–10 bunches of your first choice randomly; then add the next variety alongside the first. Again, never work into the middle of spaces.

When the project is complete, pay attention to its position. A pair of trees on a long cabinet against a wall can give a smart, formal look, especially when favourite items are carefully arranged around them. Two matching topiaries will look their best above a fireplace. If it's a real open fire, choose materials that will stand the warmth and can be fairly frequently cleaned. Avoid delicate flowers. Remember to turn the pieces regularly; this will ensure that they fade evenly and, as with all dried flowers, keep them out of direct sunlight. Damp and the sun are their worst enemies.

YOU WILL NEED:

Materials:
container
setting clay
tree trunk
florist's dry foam
foam sphere
glue

1 Fill the base of the pot with a handful of the setting clay, enough to make a layer about 2.5 cm (1 in) thick.

2 Push the bottom of the tree trunk into the clay, in the centre of the pot. As long as it is in the centre, the trunk doesn't have to be completely upright.

3 Cut some clay and roll it into sausage shapes. Pack them around the base of the trunk, pushing them down and filling the space between the sides of the pot and the tree trunk. Repeat this process until at least half the depth of the pot has been filled. Put the pot to one side and leave the clay to set hard. This may take several hours, depending on temperature and humidity; a large pot can take two days. When dry, the formed base can easily be lifted out of the pot. If you are keen to get started on the display, support the trunk with foam pushed firmly all around it, to fill the remaining half of the pot.

4 The easiest method for fixing the materials to the trunk is to use a foam sphere. Push the sphere down on to the top of the trunk, until it feels firmly fixed. Then remove the sphere, blow away any loose foam particles from the top of the trunk and the hole in the foam. Place a spot of glue on the end of the trunk and push the sphere back into position.

CHICKEN WIRE SWAG

This method is used for the base of many of the swag designs in this book, and for the floral mirror and picture frames. It is a particularly useful way of creating a swag base, because it makes a large surface to work with, if the materials are chunky or you need to cover a large area.

Materials:
chicken wire
sphagnum moss
short stub (floral)
  wires

Tools:
cutters
pliers

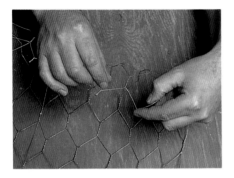

1 Carefully cut the required length and width of chicken wire, folding in the sharp edges. To cover a picture frame you will need to make four moss swags, one for each side of the picture frame.

2 Fill the centre of the wire mesh along its length with a covering of sphagnum moss as evenly as possible.

3 Fold the long edges into each other, creating a sausage shape, and with short stub (floral) wires, join them together. At this stage, you may need to remove or add some moss, so that the shape is as even as possible.

4 If you are making a base for a swag, use one or two short stub wires to make a hanger for the finished work. Simply push the wire(s) through the chicken wire and twist the two ends together to create a loop.

TIPS FOR MAKING BUNCHED SWAGS

- Build up the decoration on the swag one variety at a time, working along the whole length, to make sure the balance of each variety is correct.
- Criss-cross the bunches in different directions, so the swag can be viewed from any angle or hung any way without showing its 'mechanics'.
- Bend any sharp ends of stub (floral) wires back into the base of the swag, so they can't scratch any surfaces, or cover the back of the swag with plastic before starting work on the front to ensure the wires stay firmly in the frame.
- Make sure the materials cover the whole surface of the swag, and not just the top. From time to time, stand well back and inspect your work to make sure there are no gaps.
- Materials can be wired in place, or glued, or both. Remember that anything stub-wired can easily be repositioned, whereas items that are glued must be in the correct place from the beginning!
- When the display is finished, check that everything is firmly attached, use the glue gun to make sure of any items that are a little loose.
- A very heavy swag tends to hang forward and show the base. The best way to deal with this is to put a few fixings along its length, to hold it in place.

STUB WIRING

This is definitely the most important skill you must master when dealing with dried flowers. Untidy or loose wiring means that material will not fit easily into small areas of foam, and later, the material will fall out of the display. Take as much time as it requires to get the technique absolutely correct.

Each bunch must look neat and tidy and the materials should be held firmly in place. Practise on a handful of stems trimmed from a bunch of fresh flowers until you have a neat, tightly wired bunch. This will save wasting expensive flowers and, although it might seem a little laborious, it will pay huge dividends in the long run.

Materials:
dried flowers
stub (floral) wires

Tools:
pliers

1 Take 4–6 stems and cut them to the length you require. Hold the stems of the flowers firmly together with one hand and pass the stub (floral) wire behind them, so that the wire and the stems are at right angles to each other. Make sure you leave the short end of the wire about 3 cm (1½ in) above the stems.

2 Hold the wire and stems together between the thumb and forefinger of one hand. Bend the long end of the wire towards you, loop it around the stems and push it away from you.

3 Still holding the stems and wire together, pull the short end of the wire up so that it lies lengthways along the stems. Now wrap the longer length of wire 3–4 times diagonally around the stems, to hold them together. The wire should be firm, but not so tight that it breaks the stems.

WIRING A CANDLE

Using mossing pins or bent stub wires is a convenient method of firmly fixing a candle into foam, and makes removing the spent candle very easy. This is not really suitable for very narrow candles as they burn too quickly to make the method worthwhile.

The combination of candles and dried material is, of course, potentially very dangerous. Never leave a display with a lighted candle burning unattended. When creating the design, always ensure that the dried materials are as far away from the candle as possible. Large, good-quality, long-burning candles are the best to use; just make sure that they are extinguished before the candle reaches the base. Fire-retardant sprays are available from good florist's, and these are well worth applying to your display to make the finished piece as safe as possible. But the golden rule is *never* leave the lit display unattended.

YOU WILL NEED:

Materials:
florist's tape
candle
mossing pins or short
 stub (floral) wires

  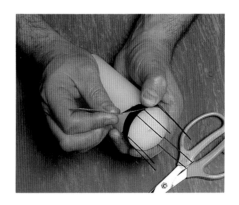

1 Wrap florist's tape at least once around the base of the candle, pulling it as tightly as possible so that the tape sticks firmly to the candle.

2 Place a mossing pin or a bent stub (floral) wire under the loose end of the tape, and cover the top of the pin or wire with the tape, again pulling it as tightly as possible so that it holds the pin in place.

3 Repeat the process so that there are at least three fixings for a small candle or six for a larger candle. Finish by pulling the tape around once more and trimming it neatly. Alternatively, use a glue gun to fix the candle in place.

MOSSING A PICTURE OR MIRROR FRAME

The basic wooden frame for this job needs to be fairly heavy, so the required fixings can get a good hold. By far the best base is a simple construction made from planed white wood, although old picture frames can be used. Avoid old frames with heavy mouldings, since these are often made of plaster and wood, and this makes getting a good fixing rather difficult.

YOU WILL NEED:

Materials:
chicken wire
sphagnum moss
short stub (floral)
  wires
wooden picture
  frame
wood screws and
  glue, if necessary
mirror glass
picture wire
fixings
hardboard or
  cardboard
tissue paper

Tools:
cutters
pliers
staple gun
bradawl (awl)

1 If the frame is a little flimsy, use wood screws and glue to strengthen it. Remember, once the frame is covered with the chicken wire and moss base, all the fixings will disappear. Make four chicken wire swags to fit the top, bottom and sides of your wooden frame. Push one swag firmly around one side of the picture frame.

2 Make sure the swag is long enough, then use a staple gun to hold it in place. Make sure that the staples trap a piece of chicken wire and hold it firmly to the wooden frame each time you fire the gun. Repeat this process along the swag every 5–8 cm (2–3 in).

To Finish: when the chicken wire and moss framework is firmly in place, turn the frame over and add the mirror glass and the hanging fixings. Remember that even a fairly small frame – without any added floral work – will be quite heavy, so make sure the fixings are very secure. Use proper, heavy-duty picture wire to hang the finished piece, and protect the back of the mirror glass with hardboard or card, so that its painted surface is not damaged. Give the glass a really good clean; this is much harder to do once the floral work is in place. Cover the glass with some tissue paper; this will further protect the surface while the materials are added. Once the project is finished, remove the tissue and blow or vacuum the debris away.

FILLING A BASKET WITH MOSS AND CHICKEN WIRE

Moss is an alternative to foam as a base. It is useful when the basket is on the large side and would require a lot of foam to do the job. However, a moss base isn't as good at holding bunches in place as a foam one, and can't be tipped upside-down.

If the basket is very large, there is no need to use moss at all; in this case the wire mesh will need to fill the whole of the basket, so that it can support the stems of the materials.

To make a chicken wire ball for a topiary tree, follow the same procedure but make the shape as spherical as possible.

YOU WILL NEED:

Materials:
large-weave chicken
  wire
basket
sphagnum moss
stub (floral) wires

Tools:
wire cutters
pliers

1 Cut a piece of large-weave chicken wire into a square approximately twice the surface area of the open top of the basket. Put an equivalent amount of moss to fill the basket, and a little more, in the centre of the wire. Fold the four corners in, creating a ball shape.

2 Push the ball into the basket, with the open, folded side underneath. Using stub (floral) wires, sew the chicken wire frame to the edge of the basket. This needs to be done about every 10 cm (4 in) around the rim.

TIPS FOR USING MOSS AS A BASE

- Always use sphagnum moss for covering and filling bases for arrangements; it's less expensive than other kinds and is easier to use, because it gives easily when you push stub (floral) wires into it.

- Moss will often be quite wet when it arrives; allow time for it to dry, out of its bag, before you begin the project, otherwise the other materials in the display may start to rot. When you've finished, allow the moss to dry out completely, especially before posting,

if you are sending the project as a gift.

- For projects using a chicken wire and moss base it is worth making the base a few days in advance, to allow it to dry out. This will also make it lighter to handle.

- Protect polished surfaces from damp moss by putting plastic sheeting underneath the display.

- Separate any compacted lumps of moss, which would be difficult to push stub (floral) wire into.

MOSS-COVERED BASKETS

This is an ideal way to make use of an old or poor-quality basket that is really only fit for the bin. Baskets, cardboard and wooden boxes of all shapes and sizes can be turned into useful display containers when covered in moss. The main disadvantage with moss is that the green colour has a fairly short life, unless it is kept well away from direct light, especially strong sunlight.

Before starting work on the outside of the basket or box, it's a good idea to fill the inside with the foam, moss or mesh. This will ensure that the outer covering is disturbed as little as possible when it comes to making the display.

YOU WILL NEED:

Materials:
reel of florist's wire
basket
dark green moss

Tools:
scissors
glue gun

1 Fix the reel wire to the basket and cover part of the basket with a good handful of moss. Wrap the wire around the basket, fastening the first handful in place. Repeat the process until the whole basket is covered, paying particular attention to the edges and the corners.

2 Tie the wire to the top edge of the basket and trim the moss evenly with scissors. Any small gaps can be filled by tucking moss under the wire; or glue moss in place using a glue gun. Again, trim away any loose pieces.

MOSS-COVERED ROPE SWAG

This is the best base for a swag to which you are going to tie the decorative materials. The covering need not be too thick; the bulk for the swag will be provided by the stems of the materials. The moss creates a good firm base to tie the material to. Don't be tempted to make the swag too short. A swag about 1 m (3 feet) long will look balanced in most projects. Many of the rules for making a swag are the same as for garlands, so it is worth reading that section for a successful finished design.

YOU WILL NEED:

Materials:	Tools:
rope	knife
stub (floral) wires	glue gun, if
reel of florist's wire	necessary
sphagnum moss	pliers

1 Cut the rope to the required length, allow enough to make a loop at each end. Use a stub (floral) wire to secure the loops or glue them if the finished piece is likely to be heavy.

2 Tie reel wire to the rope and wrap the wire around a good handful of moss, keeping the rope in the centre of the moss. Work along the whole length of the rope base until it is completely covered with moss.

MOSS- & ROPE- EDGED BASKET

Using a basic swag base in this way can actually extend the edge of the basket, making it much easier to fix other materials in position. If preferred, the swag can also be made using hay, but then the extra material must be fixed on to the swag and not into it. This is also the case with the moss and rope base (see above).

YOU WILL NEED:

Materials:	Tools:
rope	knife
stub (floral) wires	glue gun, if
reel of florist's wire	necessary
sphagnum moss	pliers
basket	

Make a moss-covered rope swag. Using stub (floral) wires, fix the rope to the edge of the basket by pushing the wire through the basket under the rope. Twist the ends together on the top. Trim off the loose ends, pushing any sharp pieces back into the moss. This will need to be done every 5–8 cm (2–3 in) right the way round the edge of the basket.

WIRING FIR CONES

A large number of cones is often required. This method is a good way of producing good, firm fixings for the cones, but you will find it hard on the hands. A good pair of pliers will help, and so will a pair of gloves and some hand cream to protect the fingers. Where bunches of cones are required, twist the stub wires together to produce the required number. When fixing the cones, it's worth putting a little glue at the base of the cones, so that they stay firmly in place.

You will need:

Materials: **Tools:**
fir cones   pliers
stub (floral) wires

1 Near the base of the cone and between its segments, wrap a stub (floral) wire all the way round. Try to find a position that allows the wire to slide under the scales of the cone.

2 Cross the two ends of the wire and carefully pull on one end until the wire is tight around the cone.

3 Twist the two ends together right along the whole length of the wire, to produce a good strong support.

CENTRE-WIRED MATERIALS

This is exactly the same technique as centre-wired bunches, but, because woody materials are often much heavier, the stub wire needs to be a little stronger to support the weight of the material. This is a perfect way for fixing cinnamon sticks and all other types of woody material, including twigs and even small branches. Once the material is in place use glue to fix it permanently. The combination of the strong stub wire and the glue will prevent even the heaviest materials from falling off the finished piece. Make sure you leave the glue long enough to dry properly before proceeding.

You will need:

Materials: **Tools:**
materials for wiring,   cutters
  e.g. cinnamon   pliers
  sticks
stub (floral) wires
ribbon, cord or raffia

1 Trim the materials to the required length. Half-way along the total length, fold the stub (floral) wire around the bunch. Hold the bunch firmly in place in one hand while the other hand folds the wire.

2 Cross the two ends over and firmly twist them together to produce a strong support. Use a pair of pliers to twist the stub wires together, to produce a stronger fixing. Take care not to break the stems under the pressure.

3 Cover the rather unattractive fixings by wrapping ribbon, cord or raffia around the bunch and tying it in a bow or knot.

CENTRE-WIRED BUNCHES

This is another basic skill that is extremely useful for many different designs. To achieve a full-looking bunch of material, put the stems together, each at a slight angle to the one before, working around the bunch. If all the stems are laid parallel, the bunch will require far more material to look as if it is a decent size. Making a swag or garland using only this method is, in many ways, far easier than tying all the materials on with reel wire, but it produces a very different look. The main advantage of this method is that you can put each bunch exactly where you want it from the start, and you need only commit it to the base when you are happy with that final position. This method uses less material, and because you can tie on the bunches facing in different directions, you can produce a rather more interesting design than when attaching bunches with reel wire, when all the bunches have to lie in the same direction.

YOU WILL NEED:

Materials: **Tools:**
dried flowers   scissors
stub (floral) wires   pliers

1 Trim the bunch to the required length. Half-way along the total length, fold the stub (floral) wire around the bunch. Hold the bunch firmly in one hand, while the other hand folds the wire.

2 Cross the two ends over and firmly twist the wires together to produce a strong support. Use a pair of pliers to twist the stub wires together, to produce a stronger fixing. Take care, when using pliers, to ensure that you don't break the stems under the pressure of the tight wire.

TIPS FOR USING WIRED BUNCHES

- If the material is heavy, strengthen the join to the frame or base with glue as well as wire, making sure that the glue comes into contact with both the material and the chicken wire frame.
- Always hold flowers by the wired area; this will help to prevent flower heads from material already added from being snapped off.
- As you push bunches into foam, use the width of your hand to open the space as much as possible. Afterwards, gently push the bunches around the new addition back into place.

WIRING LEAVES

Leaves such as magnolia often arrive with little or no stem. This technique creates a stem to work with so that you can make bunches. When you are trimming the leaf, make sure you only trim away enough to fix the stub wire to. This is a useful technique if only part of the leaf is required, or if the stalk-end of the leaf needs to show in the display, and not the pointed end.

YOU WILL NEED:

Materials: **Tools:**
leaves   scissors
stub (floral) wires   pliers

1 Trim the bottom third of the leaf away on one side of the stalk. Repeat the process on the other side, leaving a thick long stem.

2 Bunch the leaves together and wire them as bunches of flowers. When bunching the leaves together, try to alter the angle of each leaf, to create a full-looking bunch.

WIRING FRUIT AND NUTS

This method is used to wire a huge range of fruits and nuts. Many fruits can be penetrated by the stub wire quite easily; nuts will need to be drilled, however, or make a hole carefully with a bradawl (awl). Take great care during this process, because the working area is very small. If possible, hold the nut in a vice (vise), so that your hands are clear of the tools.

If the base is firm, that is, made from chicken wire and moss or woody stems, use a glue gun and fix the fruit or nuts directly in place. This is a much faster method than wiring and generally you can fix the items exactly where you want them.

YOU WILL NEED:

Materials:
dried fruit and nuts
stub (floral) wire

Tools:
bradawl (awl) or
  drill
pliers
vice (vise)

1 If necessary, make a hole through the base of the dried fruit. Push a stub (floral) wire all the way through so that an even amount of wire comes out of either side.

2 Cross the two ends and twist them together to form a strong support.

STEAMING ROSES

This simple technique can greatly improve the appearance of dried roses which are imported in large boxes with up to 25 bunches per box. Frequently some or all of the bunches arrive at their destination rather squashed. This process will give them a new lease of life but take care. Never try to open the very centre of the rose which is often discoloured. The process also works very well for peonies, but, again, great care must be taken not to open the flower too much.

YOU WILL NEED:

Materials:
kettle
dried roses

1 Bring a kettle to the boil. Hold the rose by its stem, head downwards, in the steam for a few seconds, until the outside petals start to waver.

2 Remove the rose from the steam and gently push back the outer petals, one by one.

3 If necessary, repeat the steaming process and continue to open the petals, working towards the centre of the rose.

TYING A PAPER BOW

Using this paper material is a quick, inexpensive and versatile method of producing a finishing trim for a display. It's now available in a large range of colours and in at least two different widths. The narrower ribbon is usually wound much tighter and it takes a lot of patience to unwind it ready for use. The broader ribbon is much easier to work with so use this wherever possible. Its matt finish takes florist's spray paint very well; it looks very effective when sprayed very lightly with a frosting of white, gold or silver, so that the base colour shows through.

YOU WILL NEED:

Materials:
paper ribbon
glue gun or stub
  (floral) wire

Tools:
scissors
pliers

1 Cut the ribbon to the required length. The simplest way to calculate the length is to pretend to make the bow before you cut, allowing a little extra for the knot. Gently tease the ribbon open so that it is completely flat and then scrunch it up again.

2 Fold the length in half and then pull the centre of the ribbon downwards so that it makes an M-shape. You should now have two loops.

3 Hold the two loops, cross them over each other, tie them in a knot and pull tightly. Adjust the size of the bow as required, by pulling on the tails.

4 Open out the ribbon so that the bow is well rounded. Fit the finished bow to the display with glue or thread a stub (floral) wire through the knot.

MAKING A FABRIC BOW

A display for a more formal setting can look very smart with a fabric bow especially if it is in a fabric that matches the decorative scheme of the room. This is a fairly easy way of creating a bow, the only limitation is the size; often a large bow will not keep its shape unless you stiffen it or add wire supports. Glue the bow into position, or, before you cover the stub wire with the final piece of fabric, add another stub wire running underneath the original. Twist the wires together to produce a support, in the same way as wiring fir cones and so on.

YOU WILL NEED:

Materials:
fabric
stub (floral) wire

Tools:
scissors
pliers
glue gun

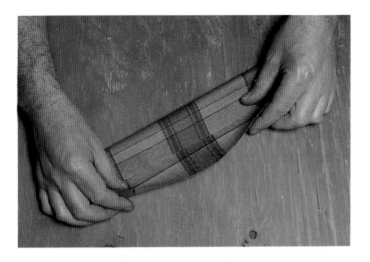

1 Fold a piece of fabric equally into three lengthways, making sure that the raw edge is not too close to one of the folded edges.

2 Fold the length again, dividing it into three so that the middle section is approximately one-third larger than the outer two.

3 Grip the fabric in the middle, pressing it into a bow shape. While holding the shape, wrap a thin stub (floral) wire around it and twist the ends together.

4 Make sure that the creases on the front of the bow are even. Twist the wires tightly together and tuck the sharp ends into the bow.

5 Fold a much smaller piece of fabric into three lengthways. It should be wide enough to look well balanced as the centre of the bow.

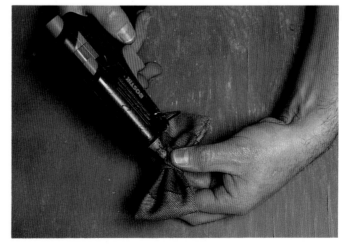

6 Wrap this around the bow, covering the stub wire. Trim the ends at the back and glue the two raw ends together, wrapping one over the top of the other. From the front the bow should have no edges showing.

Spring

A wonderful range of materials is available during this beautiful season,

in a selection of pale, gentle colours. Throughout the chapter

many different types of arrangements are presented,

all of them reflecting Spring's soft colours.

SPRING BOXED FLORAL "JUMP"

This simple display can be made in a variety of boxes; even a cardboard box can look good if it is covered with spray paint or disguised with a fabric covering. For a very rustic feel, use a wooden crate. The small one used for this display had been filled with jars of preserves and was too good to throw away. Bay leaves are best fresh from the bush as there is less risk of the leaves falling off the stems and their fresh vibrant colour can be enjoyed. When they are completely dry, their appearance will be improved with a covering of florist's spray lacquer.

YOU WILL NEED:

Materials:
florist's dry foam
  block
a wooden crate
green moss
Protea compacta
bay leaves
mossing (floral) pins
rope

Tools:
knife
cutters

1 Trim a block of foam so that it is a little smaller than the crate. Place the foam in the crate and pack any spaces with moss. Tease some of the moss through gaps in the crate so that it hangs out.

2 Trim the stems of the *Protea compacta* so that they are the required height, allowing at least 3 cm (1½ in) of the stem to penetrate the foam. Starting slightly off-centre, add a row of protea to the foam.

3 Add the second row to one side of the first, so that the two rows fill the centre of the display.

4 Trim the stems of the bay leaves and push these into the foam, making sure that the tops of the leaves are just below the bottom of the protea heads.

5 Add a collar of leaves all around the edge, completely covering the foam base. Trim with more moss, fixing it in place with mossing (floral) pins. Tie the rope loosely in place, wrapping it round a couple of times and finishing with a knot or bow.

SPRING BOX

This is a way of using gift boxes that are just too good to throw away. In this arrangement, I have used an oval box; most shapes and sizes are suitable. The candle shown is an option; a bigger box may need more than one candle to give the finished display a balanced look. The trim on the outside of the box could be changed; using a wide ribbon and bow will give a softer look.

YOU WILL NEED:

Materials:
selection of leaves
cardboard box
florist's dry foam
    block
candle
2 bunches of
    miniature pink
    roses
moss
mossing (floral) pins
raffia

Tools:
glue gun
knife
cutters
glue gun
scissors

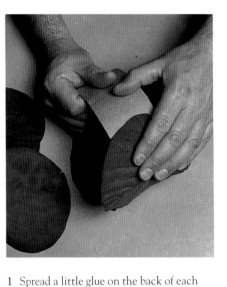

1 Spread a little glue on the back of each leaf and press the leaf firmly on to the side of the box. If the leaves are not large enough to cover the depth of the box, start the first row of leaves at the top and cover the bottom of the previous row with the next. Place the top row of leaves so that they extend well above the lip of the box.

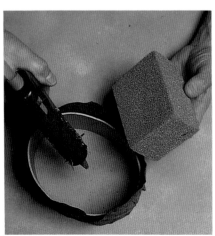

2 Trim the foam block with the knife, apply glue to the base and push it firmly into the box. Try to create a good, tight fit; this will help to ensure that the box keeps its shape.

3 When the glue has set, push the candle into the foam in the centre of the box. Then remove the candle and put a little glue into the hole. Replace the candle. This will ensure that the candle is safe. The candle stub is easily removed by twisting gently, remember to glue the new candle in.

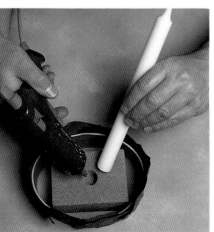

4 Trim the roses so that the finished length will allow around 3 cm (1½ in) to be pushed into the foam, and around 5 cm (2 in) above the leaves. Start inserting the roses around the outside edge of the box, spacing them to make sure the whole surface is covered. Leave a space around the candle so that there is no risk of the flowers burning. Fill any space with moss, attached with pins. Trim the moss around the candle.

5 Tie raffia around the outside of the box.

OREGANO TOPIARY TREE

Many of the materials used in dried-flower displays will slowly fade over a period, especially if they are subjected to bright light. Oregano, however, retains both its colour and its beautiful scent well. This makes it an ideal material to use for a larger project, since you will not have to consign the display to the dustbin for a very long time.

YOU WILL NEED:

Materials:
terracotta
flowerpot
setting clay
about 40 cm (15 in)
    length of tree trunk
8–10 cm (5–6 in)
    diameter florist's
    dry foam sphere
stub (floral) wire
reindeer moss
mossing (floral) pins
8–10 bunches of
    oregano

Tools:
knife
glue gun
cutters
pliers

1 Prepare and make the topiary base. Fix the reindeer moss all around the base of the tree trunk in the top of the terracotta pot, using the mossing (floral) pins. Now leave the base to dry and harden; allow at least ten hours. When the base is dry, lift it out and put glue around the inside of the pot. Replace the clay base.

TIP BOX
If you decide to make a pair of trees, always create the two bases at the same time, to ensure they are the same height. Wherever possible, use identical materials too, so that they match each other. If you use terracotta pots, you may need to cover the base with felt to prevent scratch damage and protect valuable surfaces.

2 Trim, bunch and wire all the oregano, keeping each bunch to no more than 10 cm (4 in) in length. Push the bunches into the foam sphere one at a time, always holding the opposite side of the sphere from the side on which you are adding the bunches. This will ensure that the foam doesn't split under too much pressure. To avoid crushing the delicate oregano leaves, hold the bunch as far down the stem as possible.

3 Keep adding bunches until the whole sphere is covered. Remember to stand back from your display to make sure that all the bunches are inserted to an even finished height. Always add bunches one next to the other, so that spaces are not created between each bunch. Turn the whole display upside-down, and, using mossing (floral) pins, completely cover the foam around the trunk with moss. This is not necessary if the display is to sit on a low table as then you will not be able to see the underneath.

LAVENDER AND MOSS BASKET

Most of the inner edge of this basket has only been covered with reindeer moss, so that plenty of useful space is left in the centre. The roses need to be glued directly on to the moss collar and not on to the reindeer moss; this will ensure that they do not become loose and fall off. Glue roses and reindeer moss on to the fixings of the lavender bundles, to hide the stub wires.

YOU WILL NEED:

Materials:
rope
stub (floral) wires
reel of florist's wire
sphagnum moss
basket
lavender
reindeer moss
mossing (floral) pins
roses

Tools:
knife
glue gun
pliers
cutters

1 Make a moss-covered rope swag for the outer edge of the basket and fix it in place with stub (floral) wires. Make the lavender into small bunches and centre-wire them. Push the ends of the stub wire lengthways into the moss. Repeat the process until three bunches cross each other at the same position. Repeat this twice, spacing the groups of bunches equally round the rim.

2 Moss the 'collar', fixing the moss firmly in place with the pins. Cover most of the moss collar but leave a few spaces.

3 Cut the rose heads from their stems and glue the heads in place on the moss collar. If the roses are fairly small, steam them first.

SPRING BUNCHED SWAG

The *Amaranthus caudatus* in this swag, with its arching, soft stems, creates the feeling of a collection of spring flowers. All the flowers chosen for this swag are fairly soft in colour, to emphasise the spring theme. Of course, both larkspur and peonies are summer flowers: very few spring flowers dry well, because of their delicate nature. Careful use of the right colours creates the right feeling, nevertheless.

YOU WILL NEED:

Materials:
chicken wire
sphagnum moss
stub (floral) wires
terracotta flowerpots
pink larkspur
blue larkspur
Achillea ptarmica
oregano
Amaranthus caudatus
yellow roses
peonies
green moss
mossing (floral) pins
raffia

Tools:
cutters
pliers
glue gun

1 Make a chicken wire swag about 1.3 m (4 ft) long. Attach the terracotta pots by passing a stub wire through the drainage hole in the base and over the rim. Pass the two ends through the chicken wire swag and twist them firmly together. Push the twisted ends back into the frame, to prevent any damage.

2 Centre-wire the larkspur, *Achillea ptarmica* and oregano. Starting with the pink larkspur, push the ends of the stub (floral) wire firmly into the frame. Work the whole length of the swag, adding only one variety at a time and criss-crossing the materials.

3 Trim the *Amaranthus caudatus*, leaving only 5 cm (2 in) of stem and stub-wire them. Add these to the frame along each edge of the swag, with a few bunches along the centre in between the other materials.

4 Put a little glue on the stems of small, wired bunches of the yellow roses and push them into the terracotta pots.

5 Cut the peony heads from the stems directly under the flower and glue these in place in groups of two or three, covering any stems or stub wires. Using the mossing (floral) pins, fix the green moss in place, in any spaces along the length of the swag. Finally, make a raffia bow and glue it in place.

SPRING CANDLE RING

Making a ring by this method, rather than using all centre-wired or stub-wired bunches will use far less material. This method works best for small pieces that are to be placed in a small space, but is best avoided if a large dramatic display is needed. The selection of material used here will cover a small garland in very little time, making this a good design for beginners.

YOU WILL NEED:

Materials:
copper garland ring
hay or moss
reel of florist's wire
4 florist's plastic
  candle holders
4 candles
stub (floral) wires
hydrangea
Achillea filipendulina
pink roses
peonies
green moss
mossing (floral) pins

Tools:
cutters
pliers
glue gun

1 Cover both sides of the copper ring with hay or moss. Push four candle holders on to the base, remove, then glue back into place. Stub-wire small bunches of hydrangea together. Push the ends of the wire into the base and glue in to place.

2 Cut the stems off the *achillea* about 5 cm (2 in) long, push them into the ring and glue them in place. Remember to cover both the outside and the inside of the ring.

TIP BOX
When the candle holders are fixed on the ring, put the candles in them first to check if they are standing straight, check again after finishing the piece, before gluing in to place.

3 Continue wiring and gluing all the other materials, until the whole ring has been covered. You can just wire the ingredients, but then the display will not be so permanent.

4 Fill any small spaces with green moss, fixing it in place with mossing (floral) pins. Remember to pay particular attention to the inner and outer edges. Glue the candles in to place in the holders.

SPRING CANDLE PILLAR

With its trunk covered in a dark green moss, this candle pillar looks stunning, and makes an ideal fresh, spring decoration for a grand dinner party. A pair of these above the fireplace or on the dinner table will add romantic atmosphere to any occasion. If you want a much larger piece, make a chicken wire frame filled with moss. Wrap this around the trunk and fill it with centre-wired or stub-wired bunches as described in Summer Chandelier. Choose a candle that balances the thickness of the floral base; if it is too thin it will make the base appear too heavy. Because of its height, this pillar is rather more vulnerable to accidents, so do make sure you display it in a secure position!

YOU WILL NEED:

Materials:
medium terracotta
  flowerpot
setting clay
tree trunk
small terracotta
  flowerpot
green moss
reel of florist's wire
yellow roses
echinops
mossing (floral) pins
tall candle

Tools:
glue gun
cutters

1 Make a topiary base, using the medium terracotta pot, clay and tree trunk. Using the glue gun, fix the small terracotta pot to the top of the trunk, making sure that it is completely straight.

2 Tuck moss into the base of the larger pot and wrap it around the trunk, tying it in place with reel wire. Keep the moss as even as possible and not too thick.

3 Continue the whole process until the whole trunk has been covered, making sure that the area around the pot at the top of the trunk also has a good layer.

4 If the rose heads are small steam them open. Trim the stems off the rose heads and glue the heads in small groups on to the moss, in various positions around the trunk.

5 Repeat the process with the echinops, until the whole surface area of the moss is covered. Fill any small gaps with green moss, fixing it in place with a glue gun or mossing (floral) pins. Fix the candle in the pot, either by gluing, or by packing the pot tightly with moss.

SEASHELL SOAP DISH

This shell had a number of small holes along its base; it was an ideal candidate for this project, because the water from the drying soap would easily drain away. The inside had a wonderful coating of mother-of-pearl, so even empty it would look quite stunning. Shells are fairly easy to drill, either by hand or with an electric drill set on slow, so you can create drainage holes if they are not there naturally. If you collect shells on holiday, make sure you don't break any local environment laws. Processed shells can be very effective, they have had the rough coat removed to reveal a beautiful iridescent layer.

Experiment with different types of moss. The most suitable is reindeer moss, because this stands up well to damp conditions. Whatever type you use keep it to the minimum as the dish will need to be washed from time to time. Glue the rope using epoxy resin, which will hold it in place far better on a very smooth surface. So that the soap does not sit in a pool of water at the bottom of the dish, put a handful of rounded shells in the base.

YOU WILL NEED:

Materials:
large shell
rope
selection of small
  shells
moss

Tools:
glue gun
scissors

TIP BOX
Take great care when using a hot glue gun with such small objects. Don't be tempted to remove hot glue from your hand until it has set; simply run cold water over the glue and then gently remove it as a solid lump.

When buying seashells, ensure that they are from a reputable source. Most are by-products of a processing stage of the food industry.

1 Put some glue into the middle of the base of the large shell. Make a rope coil and press it firmly into the glue, before it begins to set hard. Continue coiling the rope around, adding glue to the shell as you work. Cover about a third of the shell, to provide a soft, stable base. Cut the rope-end at a sharp angle and glue this to the edge of the coil, to finish it.

2 Turn the shell over and glue another piece of rope in place all round the outer edge. If the shell is wide enough, repeat to provide a lip on which to fix small shells.

3 Put some glue on the rope and press the first small shell firmly in place. Continue this process, working around the dish. Add the larger shells first and then return to the spaces and fill them with the smaller shells. Glue the shells, not just on the rope, but to each other, creating an even "collar". Fill any gaps with tiny pieces of glued moss.

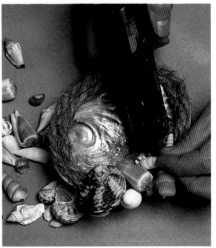

COUNTRY BASKET

This kind of basket display will make the most of your stub-wiring skills. Working with lots of material in a fairly small space dictates that the wiring must be as neat as possible, to ensure that all the stems fit into the small foam base. Dried flowers are available at all times of the year, of course, but the selection chosen for this basket lends itself to a spring appearance, especially with the addition of *Amaranthus caudatus* around the edges.

YOU WILL NEED:

Materials: **Tools:**

florist's dry foam   knife
  block   cutters
round basket
sphagnum moss
amaranthus
oregano
larkspur
miniature pink rose
pale green
  Amaranthus
  caudatus
stub (floral) wires
green moss
mossing (floral) pins

1 Use a sharp knife to trim the foam into shape, making sure that it fits snugly into the basket. Leave about 2.5 cm (1 in) between the top of the basket and the foam. Pack sphagnum moss between the edge of the basket and the foam to keep it firmly in place.

2 Separate all the bunches of flowers and trim to about 20 cm (8 in) long. Place each separated bunch on the work surface. Wire each variety into small bunches. Starting with the least fragile flowers, push the stems into the foam. Add one variety at a time, using the oregano as the main filler.

3 Build up the display, saving the roses and amaranthus till last. The aim is to create a well filled display, with little or no space between the different bunches.

4 Attach the roses and lastly the
Amaranthus caudatus, pushing it into the
foam around the edge of the basket so that
it hangs down to touch the surface.

5 Use the green moss and mossing (floral)
pins to trim the edge of the basket generously.
Make sure that no foam is showing.

Summer

The summer months produce an abundance of fresh material, suitable for
drying at home, which can be collected from the garden or the countryside.
Many of these ingredients can be used in the Summer arrangements to create
stunning, colourful displays that will look good throughout the season.

SUMMER FLORAL "JUMP"

This display has been made with a flat back, so that it can stand against a wall or in a small fireplace. If it is to be seen from all sides, the process is almost exactly the same, but the first two rows of flowers need to start in the centre, and not at one edge. Then add the other flowers, working all the way around. If you need a larger display, simply glue several blocks of foam together; keep the leaves as high as possible, so they do not cover the fabric sides.

YOU WILL NEED:

Materials:
cardboard
florist's dry foam
  block
fabric
mossing (floral) pins
peonies
stub (floral) wires
lavender
Alchemilla mollis
cobra leaves
raffia
green moss

Tools:
scissors
glue gun
cutters
pliers

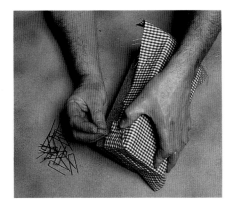

1 Cut a piece of cardboard to fit the bottom of the foam block and glue it in place. Lay the foam block on the fabric and cut a piece large enough to cover the bottom and wrap up the sides by about 5 cm (2 in). Hold the sides of the fabric in place with mossing pins, making sure that the base of the fabric is crease-free.

2 Trim the peony stems to the desired length. Starting at the back of the display, push two rows into the foam block, leaving space at either end to add the other materials. Make sure that at least 3 cm (1½ in) of the stem penetrates the foam. Do not put material right at the edge of the foam; it will break away.

3 Bunch and wire the lavender and push into the foam, along the front and sides of the peonies so that the tops of the lavender are level with the bottoms of the peonies. Repeat the same process for the *Alchemilla mollis,* so that their tops are level with the bottoms of the lavender.

4 Fix the cobra leaves along the front and the sides of the display with mossing pins; wrap at least one leaf around the back corners of the display. Keep them as high as possible, so they don't cover the fabric sides.

5 Tie a hank of raffia around the arrangement, to cover the mossing pins. As an alternative to the raffia trim, consider a fabric bow of the same material as the base. Tuck green moss in the back to cover any foam that is showing.

VARIATION ON
FLORAL "JUMP"

A floral jump can be made from a
huge range of different materials,
to suit all the seasons of the year.
The materials chosen for this display
will keep their colours, even through
the bright summer months, although
you should keep them away from
direct sunlight. Dark red roses and
lavender are particularly good in
stronger light. The roses have been
steamed, so that fewer are required to
cover the area. The cinnamon-stick
collar around the base has been glued
on to cardboard fixed in place with
mossing pins. The tartan bow and
trim gives the impression of holding
the cinnamon-sticks in place.

SUMMER CANDLE-CUFF

Choose a tall, wide candle for this project, so that the cuff is large enough to apply the dried flower materials. The candle must be at least twice the height of the cuff, so that it has plenty of room to burn without any danger of setting the hessian (burlap) alight. Make sure the candle is well wrapped before the start of the project to ensure that the candle is kept clean and that the hot glue will not melt the wax as it is applied to the paper base and hessian.

YOU WILL NEED:

Materials:
thick brown paper
candle
clear tape
  (cellophane)
hessian (burlap)
rope
twigs
stub (floral) wire
moss
6 roses

Tools:
scissors
glue gun
pliers
cutters

TIP BOX

This project does require a little patience, but once you have mastered the basic skill, you can use many different materials to decorate the cuff, such as seashells, starfish and reindeer moss for a bathroom; or a woody combination, such as cones and dried mushrooms, for winter. Remember that leftover bits and pieces from other displays will probably be enough for a candle cuff, so keep leftovers in a box for future experiments.

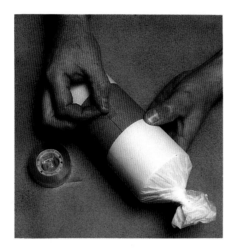

1 Cut a piece of brown paper approximately 8 cm (3 in) wide and long enough to wrap around your chosen candle. Tape the loose end down; the paper collar must be able to move freely up and down the candle.

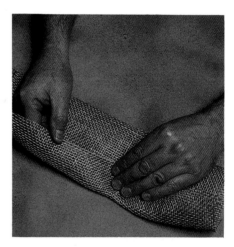

2 Cut a piece of hessian (burlap) twice as wide as the paper and long enough to wrap round the candle. Fold the two outer quarters up to meet in the middle and glue them down.

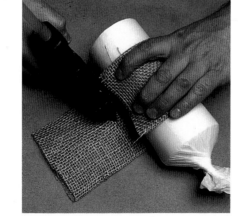

3 Lay the candle on the wrong side of the fabric and apply a little glue on either side of the candle. Wrap the fabric tightly around the candle, smoothing it to fit the paper neatly, and applying glue where necessary.

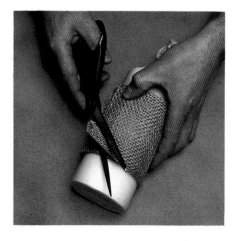

4 Trim the corners of the exposed edge and glue them down sparingly.

5 Wrap the rope around the hessian cuff once and hold it in place. Apply glue all the way around the rope, so that the glue comes into contact with both the rope and the hessian. Wrap the rope around the candle again, as close as possible to the first wrap, pushing it into the hot glue. Repeat the process until the whole of the cuff has been covered.

6 Make a small bundle of twigs and centre-wire it. Glue the bundle and some green moss to the cuff at an angle, using the moss to cover the wire that holds the twigs together. Cut the heads from the roses and glue them in place around the twigs.

SUMMER ROSE BUNDLE

This project uses the same technique as the autumn variation; the colour, ingredients, and the look are completely different. This bright, compact arrangement would be a welcome gift for someone unwell at home or in hospital, with the advantage that a display this size will take very little precious bedside space. You could also make the display with the flower stems very short, and push a tall candle into the middle of the foam. A dinner table with an individual rose bundle for each place looks very welcoming. As always, never leave candles burning unattended and remove the candle before it burns down to the top of the dried material.

YOU WILL NEED:

Materials:
florist's dry foam
  round
brown paper
stub (floral) wires
pink larkspur
pink roses
cobra or similar
  leaves
mossing (floral) pins
raffia
moss

Tools:
glue gun
sharp craft knife or
  scalpel
pliers
cutters
scissors

1 Place the foam round in the centre of the brown paper and glue it in place. Use a knife or scalpel to make cuts from the edge of the foam to the outer edge of the paper, working all the way around at roughly 1 cm (½ in) intervals.

2 Fold up the paper strips to wrap the foam. Twist a stub (floral) wire around the paper and the foam. Before twisting the two ends together too tightly, make sure all the paper strips are straight and neat at the base. Trim the paper in line with the foam.

3 Prepare and cut the larkspur and rose stems, retaining as many of the leaves as possible. Starting in the centre, push them one at a time into the foam.

4 Continue the process until the whole of the foam has been covered with larkspur and roses. If you want more leaf in the display, wire some bunches of rose leaves together and stick these into the foam.

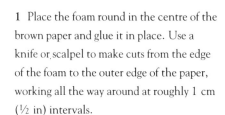

5 Wrap three or four cobra leaves around the base, fixing each one in place with a mossing (floral) pin. Make sure each pin is placed at the same height as the last.

6 Wrap a stub wire around the leaves at the same level as the pins and twist the two ends together to make a tight fixing.

7 Trim the leaves at the base of the display with scissors, so that the display will stand evenly without wobbling.

8 Tie raffia around the base, covering all the fixings. Finish with a bow or a simple knot. If the roses had a limited number of leaves, fill the spaces around the stems with moss, to hide the foam.

SUMMER TABLE SWAG

A rich, colourful collection of flowers has been used to create this summer table swag; combined with fresh fruit and candles, this arrangement is ideal for a summer-evening dinner in the garden. You can open the larkspur by holding it in steam for a few seconds, to lift the creases from the petals.

YOU WILL NEED:

Materials:
wheat
oregano
Eucalyptus spiralus
pink larkspur
peonies
pink roses
reel of florist's wire
rope
selection of candles
terracotta flowerpots
green moss
fresh fruit

Tools:
cutters
glue gun
kettle

1 Separate all the stems of the various bunches of flowers, trim them to about 15–20 cm (6–8 in) and make a pile of each variety, excluding the peonies and roses. Starting with the wheat, bind the materials to the rope in small bunches with reel wire.

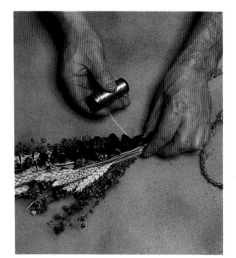

2 Continue to cover the rope in this manner, evenly spacing the materials along its entire length. Make sure that the materials are evenly spaced and that some of the material trails on to the work surface as it is tied to the rope.

3 Choose the ingredients carefully, so that a good balance of colour and form is achieved. Remember that the brighter colours, such as the pink of the larkspur, will stand out more from the swag than the darker colours.

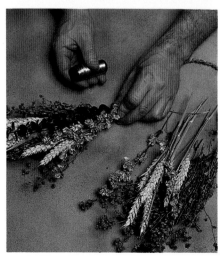

4 Steam the roses and peonies to make them as open as possible. Cut the stems from the peony- and rose-heads and glue them to the swag, spacing them evenly along the whole length. Arrange the candles in pots, placing moss and fruit freely to cover all the fixings.

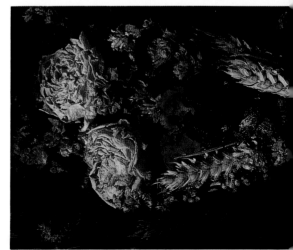

SUMMER LEAF-CIRCLE PLACE SETTING

These unusual table decorations are very simple and quick to make. Any type of leaf – or even a combination – will do, I have used cobra leaves because not many are needed to create the circle. Because it is a small design, the flowers for the leaf cones are leftovers from other displays; if you intend to make enough circles for a dinner party, use a whole bunch of one or two varieties, so that they all match. Place the circle so that the flowers are facing across the table then the guest on the opposite side will enjoy the decoration to the full.

YOU WILL NEED:

Materials:
plate
brown paper
pencil
cobra leaves
stub (floral) wires
miniature roses
larkspur

Tools:
scissors
glue gun
cutters
pliers

1 Place a plate on a piece of paper, draw a circle around it and cut it out. Put the first leaf on the paper, with the tip overlapping the edge. Put some glue on the leaf near the edge and lay the second leaf on the glue. Repeat this process until the whole circle has been created.

2 Make a cobra leaf into a cone shape and glue the edge so that it keeps its shape. Do this three times.

3 Glue the first two cones on to the leaf circle. Place the third cone on top of the first two and glue it in position.

4 Wire three small bunches of flowers and gently push them into the cones.

QUICK SEASIDE TABLE ARRANGEMENT

The aim of the first part of this project is to give height and structure to the display; it will not have the same impact if everything is on one level. There are no strict rules for this design, here the feeling is very much of the seaside; the same collection could be used on a table on the beach, for an informal buffet or even for a grand beach picnic. When the occasion is over, all the materials can be packed away for another time.

YOU WILL NEED:

Materials:	Tools:
florist's dry foam block	knife
various types of moss,	cutters
including reindeer,	pliers
tilancia and green	scissors
moss	
mossing (floral) pins	
stub (floral) wires	
Eryngium alpinum	
yellow roses	
raffia	
terracotta flowerpots	
candles	
starfish	
shells	

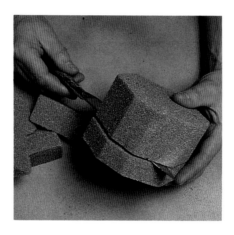

1 Trim the foam with the knife to produce a base large enough to stand a large terracotta pot on.

2 Surround the base of the pot and sides of the foam with green moss, fixing it in place with mossing (floral) pins.

3 Trim and centre-wire the bunches of eryngium and push the ends of the wires into the foam base. Place one bunch on each side of the foam.

4 Repeat the process with the roses, trimming them with raffia to cover the wire twisted around each bunch. Move the arrangement to its final position. Place as many candle pots around the centrepiece as you like and fill the spaces in between with the selection of mosses.

TIP BOX

Whether the table is long and thin or round, echo its shape with the way the moss and candles are arranged. Place all the other ingredients in and around the candles and moss, so that they cascade away from the centre.

SUMMER FLORAL MIRROR

This is a fairly adventurous project, but if you have plenty of time and lots of space to make a mess it is well worth the effort. To gain as much confidence as possible, it is a good idea to make a fairly small piece first, or make one or two bunched swags and candle rings. The basic method for making these is exactly the same as for the mirror but on a much smaller scale, and this will help you to get a feel for this method of working.

YOU WILL NEED:

Materials:
chicken wire
sphagnum moss
substantial wooden
  frame with mirror
stub (floral) wires
selection of flowers,
  including yellow
  and red roses,
  solidago, peonies,
  lavender, wheat,
  Achillea ptarmica,
  alpine eryngium
  and poppies
mushrooms
cinnamon sticks
pomegranates
terracotta flowerpots
green moss

Tools:
strong cutters
pliers
glue gun
scissors

To Start: make the chicken wire swags to make a frame. If the sphagnum moss is very damp, make the frame a few days before. Attach the frame to the wooden frame. You may find it helpful to fit the mirror glass before the addition of any flowers but after the moss framework has been fixed in place, to reduce the risk of smashing the mirror while using the staple gun. The back of the mirror will need a backing sheet so the painted surface does not get scratched. Bunch and centre-wire, all the materials, trimming them to a length of about 15 cm (6 in).

1 Push a stub (floral) wire through each terracotta pot and over its rim, and then push the loose ends into the moss frame, twisting the loose ends together when they appear on the other side of the framework. Begin attaching the decorative materials one at a time, spacing each evenly around the frame. In the early stages, push the loose ends of the stub wires through the frame and twist them together. If the material does not feel firmly attached, glue the stub wire to the chicken wire frame.

2 Continue until nearly all the frame has been covered. Completely remove the stems of some of the items, such as some poppies and roses, and then either glue them directly on to the framework, or glue them over the stub wires of centre-wired ingredients. Make sure the glue is in contact with the wire as well as the moss. Always work with one variety at a time, adding several small bunches in one place to create a strong impact. Make sure that each ingredient is evenly distributed throughout the frame.

3 Finally, when all the materials are securely attached, trim the frame with the green moss, using mossing pins to hold it in place. Pay particular attention to the edges that hang nearest to the wall, which, because it is underneath while you are working, is often forgotten when the frame is flat on the work surface.

To Finish: take great care to make the hanging fixings for the mirror as strong as possible; if you can, use a proper frame steel or a very strong rope tied to very strong steel eyes. The combination of glass, wood, damp moss and dried material can be extremely heavy. If the moss is still damp when the project is finished, hang it in a warm, dry place. Never wrap it in any form of plastic, because this will encourage the growth of mould. In time the materials will need cleaning with a soft brush and a hairdryer set on cold.

SMALL SEASHORE SWAG

This swag has been made very flexible so you can hang it easily in different locations. Here it's hanging on a glass door so that it can be seen from both sides, but it would be just as effective around a plain bathroom mirror. Instead of the small branches, you could use driftwood collected from the beach. Small pebbles are an alternative to starfish. Make sure, when gluing the items in place, that none of the dry glue shows; use different types of moss to hide any glue, as well as to provide different textures. All the materials used on this swag will stand up to the conditions found in a bathroom; do take care if you decide to use alternatives, because dried flowers will suffer in damp conditions. Preserved materials will generally stand dampness better.

YOU WILL NEED:

Materials:
rope
starfish
tilancia moss
eucalyptus
stub (floral) wires
shells
lichen moss
small branches

Tools:
glue gun
scissors
cutters

1 Cut a length of rope 1–1.3 m (3–4 ft) long. Randomly tie knots along its length and make a loop at one end.

2 Glue one side of a starfish and lay the rope across it.

3 Glue a second starfish over the top of the first, trapping the rope between the two. Tuck some tilancia moss around the edges of the two starfish, so that some of it hangs out of the sides. Repeat this process at several points along the rope.

4 Cut the eucalyptus to 20 cm (8 in) lengths. Using stub (floral) wires, fix several pieces to the rope in one place. Repeat this along the rope about every 25 cm (10 in).

5 Glue a shell at the base of the eucalyptus bunches. Work around the rope until the bases of the stems and the stub wires have been covered. Trim with a little lichen moss and repeat the process along the whole length of the rope at varying intervals, using all the shells, starfish and small branches.

SUMMER CHANDELIER

This striking chandelier is made in a similar way as the Autumn Candle Ring. The arrangement has been designed to hang fairly low over a table, so no flowers have been added to the base. If the chandelier needs to hang higher, turn the display over so that it sits on the rims of the pots, and cover the base with flowers in the same way. When the base is finished, tie the ropes to the hanging points before moving it, so you can hang it up without resting it the right way up again, to avoid crushing the flowers underneath. This particular mix of flowers will keep its colours for a long time, but you may need to replace the moss after a few months, because the green colour is always the first to fade.

YOU WILL NEED:

Materials:
flat or standard
  copper garland ring
florist's dry foam
4 terracotta
  flowerpots
sphagnum moss
reel of florist's wire
stub (floral) wires
blue and pink
  larkspur
roses
Achillea ptarmica
peonies
dark green moss
mossing (floral) pins
4 hanging ropes
4 candles

Tools:
cutters
glue gun
pliers

1 Make a flat copper ring, following step 1 of Autumn Candle Ring. Glue a small block of foam under the ring and to a terracotta pot, making sure that at least one of the copper wires crosses the centre of the foam, changing the angle of the wire if necessary. Fix the four pots equally round the ring.

2 When the glue has set, wrap sphagnum moss around the copper ring, holding it in place with reel wire. The layer needs to be about 2.5 cm (1 in) thick. Pay particular attention to the base of the ring, making sure that the foam base and the area around the pots is covered.

3 Push both ends of a thick, strong stub (floral) wire through the ring, between two pots on the inner edge. Make sure that it crosses the copper frame under the moss. Twist the two ends together and tuck the ends back into the moss. The hanging cord will be attached to this loop of wire.

4 Make centre-wired bunches of the larkspur, roses and *Achillea ptarmica*, pushing the tail of the stub wire into the moss frame. Angle the material from the inside of the frame to the outside.

5 Continue adding the various materials, criss-crossing them and making sure that the outer and inner edges of the ring are also covered. Fix the materials in the same order in each quarter of the ring, to give balance to the whole design.

6 Cut the stems off the peonies. Glue the peony heads into place, then, with the mossing (floral) pins attach the dark green moss to the ring. Again, pay particular attention to the sides of the ring, using the moss to fill any spaces between the flowers. Attach the hanging ropes and then fit the candles into the pots, using foam and moss.

TIP BOX

Remember that when the chandelier is up, you will be viewing it at a different angle from when you are making it. Keep this in mind while attaching the materials, and even hold it up every so often to see how it looks from below.

FIREPLACE DISPLAY

This is one of the very best projects for a beginner. It is an extremely simple design to make, and has the advantage that you can re-make it as many times as necessary to create the right look, without damaging any of the ingredients. This particular display has been made to look the same from all angles. Even though it is for a fireplace it can be turned occasionally, so that it fades evenly; and you can take it out of the fireplace in winter and put it in another position. A fireplace display will get more dusty than others. Clean with a hairdryer set on cold, and finish with a soft brush. Some of the flowers may break with this treatment, but you can replace damaged stems without disturbing the whole of the display.

YOU WILL NEED:

Materials:
chicken wire
basket
amaranthus
pink larkspur
pink and red roses
lavender

1 Cut a piece of chicken wire approximately twice the surface area of the basket. Scrunch it up and push it into the basket, filling the whole of the inside.

2 Separate all the bunches of flowers and discard any waste. Starting with the amaranthus, push a few stems into the basket, through the wire mesh to the bottom. Use this material as the filler. There should be enough in the basket to cover most of the top of the wire mesh, leaving space for the other ingredients.

3 Arrange the larkspur in the spaces between. Stand back from the display to check that the balance is correct.

4 Add the roses and lavender. Make sure to put some rose heads low down at the front of the basket for added interest. Place the display on the floor and check from all angles that the balance is correct.

VARIATION ON FIREPLACE DISPLAY

In this fireplace display variation, the basket is very large and the back has been filled with logs to add a different texture to the finished arrangement. The basic design is the same and the same techniques are used to build the finished piece.

Yet the mood of the piece is completely different; the softer colours of the pale pink roses and peonies are combined with solidago and wheat, which, over a period of time, will change from pale pink to golden brown. The raffia bow gives the display a feel of the countryside.

LARGE SEASIDE SWAG

This swag is made from a collection of materials that make it ideal for the damp conditions of a bathroom. If you decide to wire the shells, first drill them with an electric drill on the lowest setting so that you can pass a stub wire through the hole and into the chicken wire frame.

YOU WILL NEED:

Materials:	**Tools:**
chicken wire	cutters
sphagnum moss	pliers
stub (floral) wires	glue gun
terracotta flowerpots	
Eryngium alpinum	
echinops	
Eucalyptus spiralus	
shells	
starfish	
mossing (floral) pins	
green moss	
reindeer moss	
yellow roses	
raffia	

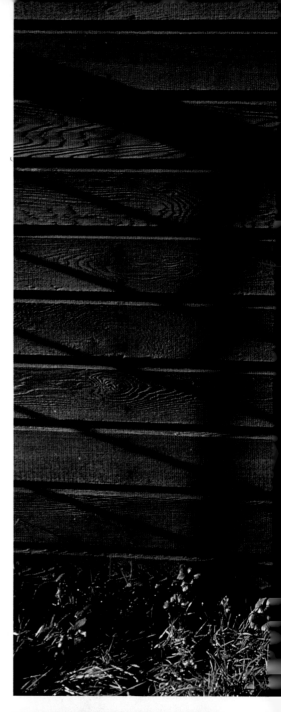

1 Make a chicken wire swag about 1.3 m (4 ft) long. Fix several terracotta pots in place along its length, by passing a stub (floral) wire through the drainage hole in the base and over the rim. Pass the ends through the chicken wire frame and twist them firmly together. Make sure that the ends are pushed back into the frame to prevent any damage.

2 Centre-wire the eryngium and push the ends of the wire firmly into the frame. Work gradually along the whole length of the swag, criss-crossing the bunches of eryngium as you go.

3 Wire small bunches of echinops or glue them directly on to the frame. Again, carefully space these along the whole length of the swag, remembering to cover both the sides and the top.

4 Repeat with the eucalyptus, spacing the bunches along the swag and around the terracotta pots.

5 Use the glue gun to fix the shells and starfish, making sure that the glue comes into contact with the chicken wire frame, the stems and the stub wires.

6 Using the mossing (floral) pins, fix the moss into any spaces along the swag. Finally, bunch the roses and push them in fours and fives into the pots. Tie the raffia into a bow and glue it to one end of the swag.

Autumn

Now is the time to remove the Summer displays from the fireplace
and go hunting for Autumn fruits from the countryside. These,
combined with some of the rich colourful materials grown in the
summer months, make wonderful combinations.

AUTUMN ROSE BUNDLE

This small display is one of the easiest to make, although it does have a fair number of steps. Roses, especially yellow or orange ones, will keep their colour for a very long time, so this makes an ideal display to fill a dark corner. Any combination of dried materials can be used. Raffia always gives a display a country feel; for a smarter location, the arrangement could be trimmed with a fabric bow.

YOU WILL NEED:

Materials:
florist's dry foam
　round
brown paper
stub (floral) wires
orange or yellow
　roses
cobra or similar
　leaves
mossing (floral) pins
raffia
moss

Tools:
glue gun
sharp craft knife or
　scalpel
pliers
cutters
scissors

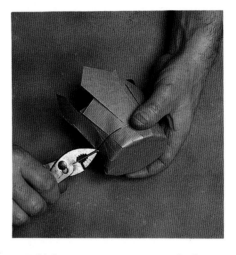

1 Place the foam round in the centre of the brown paper and glue it in place. Cut from the edge of the foam to the outer edge of the paper, working all the way around at roughly 1 cm (½ in) intervals.

2 Fold the paper strips up to wrap the foam. Wrap a stub (floral) wire round the paper and the foam, making sure all the paper strips are straight and neat at the base, and twist the two ends of the wire tightly together.

3 Trim the paper in line with the top of the foam. Prepare and cut the rose stems, retaining as many leaves as possible. Starting in the centre, push them carefully, one at a time, into the foam.

4 Continue the process until the whole of the foam has been covered with roses. About twelve roses should be enough to fill the space. If more leaves are required in the display, wire some bunches together and add them to the foam.

5 Wrap three to four cobra leaves around the base, fixing each one in place with a mossing (floral) pin. Make sure you place each pin at the same height as the last.

6 Wrap a stub wire around the leaves at the same level as the mossing (floral) pins and twist the ends together to make a tight fixing.

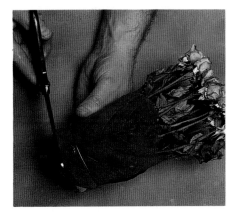

7 Trim the leaves at the base of the display with scissors, so that it will stand evenly.

8 Tie raffia around the base, covering all the fixings, and finish with a bow or a simple knot. If the roses had a limited number of leaves, fill the spaces around the stems with moss, to hide the foam.

COUNTRY BASKET

This is a classic country basket, using some of the best dried flowers. A huge range of colour mixtures is possible, but this display is an interesting alternative to the usual autumnal oranges, using a rich, dark mixture that shows the best of summer with a strong hint of winter. To give the display a more traditional autumn appearance, simply add a little yellow, such as *Alchemilla mollis*, and some dark brown, preserved oak leaves. When creating a display for this time of the year, choose a fairly dark, sturdy basket; many are simply too light to suit the finished display.

YOU WILL NEED:

Materials:
florist's dry foam
  block
large round or oval
  basket
tilancia moss and/or
  hay
larkspur
red amaranthus
oregano
blue *eryngium*
  alpinum
red roses
peonies
stub (floral) wires
mossing (floral) pins

Tools:
sharp knife
cutters
pliers

1 Use the knife to trim the foam into shape, making sure that it fits snugly into the basket. Leave at least 2.5 cm (1 in) between the top of the basket and the foam. If your basket is very deep, simply leave the stems of the flowers longer. Make sure that the foam is not visible near the edge of the basket. Pad any spaces with moss or hay.

2 Separate all the bunches of flowers and trim them so that they are approximately 25 cm (10 in) long. Place each separated bunch on the work surface. Starting with the least fragile flowers, wire them into bunches. Push them into the foam, creating an S-shape with each variety across the basket, working from one side to the other.

3 Build up the display, saving the roses and peonies until last. The aim is to create a well filled display, with little or no space between the different bunches, so that all the ingredients seem to flow into one another, with no harsh lines between materials.

4 Add the roses and peonies, distributing them evenly across the basket.

5 Now work around the edge of the basket, adding the moss so that as much foam and as many stems are hidden as possible. Hold the moss in place with mossing (floral) pins. Let the moss hang down the side, to give a soft look to the edge of the basket.

FLOWER-EDGED AUTUMN BASKET

This is a very grand piece, using a rich collection of materials to produce an eye-catching piece that will retain its good looks for a long time. All the ingredients in this basket will keep their colour well; the only one that won't last long is the green moss, but this can easily be replaced. Particular care needs to be taken when building this display, so that the materials form an even, well balanced collar. Although a glue gun has been used here to fix some of the items, all of them can be wired in place; this will add to the time it takes to finish the display.

YOU WILL NEED:

Materials:	Tools:
copper garland ring	pliers
sphagnum moss	cutters
reel of florist's wire	glue gun
round basket	
stub (floral) wires	
eucalyptus	
tolbos	
red roses	
marjoram	
pomegranates	
hydrangeas	
green moss	
mossing (floral) pins	

1 Flatten a copper ring and cover it with sphagnum moss, attached with reel wire (see Autumn Candle Ring). Fix the ring to the top of the basket with stub (floral) wires. If the copper ring is the wrong size, make a moss-covered swag rope and fix this to the top of the basket with stub wire. Divide the ring into quarters, and allocate a quarter of the ingredients to each. Trim and centre-wire the eucalyptus into bunches and push the ends of the wire into the moss, ensuring that the bunches always cross from the outside to the inside of the ring.

2 Trim the roses and marjoram and centre-wire them in the same way. Add them to the ring, criss-crossing them over the eucalyptus and each other. Make sure the bunches cover the inside and outer edge of the ring.

TIP BOX

This is a useful piece to have around the home. Left empty it is simply decorative, but for a quick dinner-table centrepiece, fill it with sweets or fresh fruit, to make a strong impact. You could also fill the centre with a collection of candle pots, but, as always, make sure they are kept well away from the flowers.

3 Glue the pomegranates into place or make a hole through each pomegranate and fix it in place with a stub wire. Bunch together some hydrangeas with a stub wire, and fix them to the base.

4 Cut off the stems of the tolbos close to the heads and glue them in place. Add these in twos and threes to provide more impact.

5 Fill any small spaces with green moss, using the mossing (floral) pins. Pay particular attention to the edges of the basket, both inside and outside.

NAPKIN RINGS

Almost any type of large, preserved leaf can be used to make these napkin rings. Preserved leaves often have dye added to the preserving liquid, which can sometimes rub off the leaf, leaving a stain. Before working with the material, give it a gentle rub with a cloth to see if this happens (the darker coloured leaves cause the most problems). Dried leaves can be used, but they are often brittle and will not last very long.

YOU WILL NEED:

Materials:
cobra leaves
red roses
green moss

Tools:
glue gun
cutters

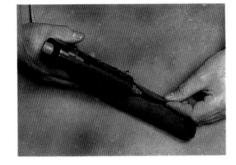

1 Roll a leaf to form a tube, glue the edge down and hold until it sets.

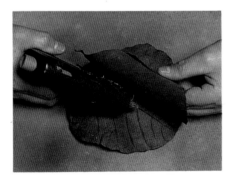

2 Glue the tube-shaped leaf to a flat leaf along its centre spine. Choose a leaf that is about the same length as the rolled leaf.

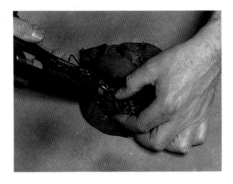

3 Either side of the rolled leaf, glue two red roses. If they are rather small, glue more than two or steam them to produce a larger flower.

4 Trim with a little green moss, fixing it in place with glue.

AUTUMN-LEAVES BOX

This idea completely transforms a very plain cardboard box. You could choose a selection of ingredients that are all edible for an unusual table centrepiece. The design shown here is more decorative, and would look very smart on a polished sideboard or cabinet, because the rich colours go well with dark furniture. For the dinner table, the centre could be filled with sugared almonds or crystallized fruit. The arrangement works well without the candle, but if the box is to be filled with exotic nibbles, the candle will add a magic touch.

YOU WILL NEED:

Materials:
florist's dry foam
  block
cardboard box
selection of preserved
  or dried leaves
raffia
reindeer moss
candle
selection of nuts and
  dried fruit
chillies
stub (floral) wires

Tools:
knife
glue gun
scissors

1 Trim the foam block to the shape of the box. Apply some glue to the base of the box and push the foam firmly into the box. Try to create a good, tight fit; this will ensure that the box keeps its shape.

2 Spread a little glue on the back of each leaf and press it firmly on to the side of the box. If the leaves are not large enough to cover the depth of the box, start the first row of leaves at the top and cover the bottom of the previous row with the next row. Place the top row of leaves so that they extend well above the lip of the box.

3 Wrap the raffia around the box and tie it in a bow.

4 Trim all the leaves that extend over the base of the box so that the box will stand flat. Take care not to split the leaves as the scissors cut them.

5 Arrange some reindeer moss inside the edge of the box, leaving the centre clear.

6 Take the candle and push it into the foam, in the centre of the box. Then remove the candle and put a little glue into the hole. Replace the candle. Remember to glue the replacement candle, when you need to change the previous one.

7 Arrange all the ingredients in the box. Make sure that a varied selection is visible, keeping the very best items, such as the dried oranges, until last.

8 Bunch and centre-wire the chillies. Tie them with raffia to cover the stub (floral) wire and then gently push the ends of the stub wire through the fruit into the foam. Depending on the size of your box, two or three bunches of chillies should be enough.

AUTUMN FABRIC AND FLOWER SWAG

With a design incorporating fabric it is extremely important to consider the final location of the display, and coordinate the fabric and flower colours with the décor, this is an ideal swag for an entrance hall or lobby. The terracotta adds a rustic, country touch to the piece, but of course it will work just as well without the pots, if you pin the swirls of fabric in place. For a prettier, lighter look, use pale coloured chintz and summer flowers, such as yellow solidago, oregano and pale yellow roses, with a little pale blue lavender; or try a mixture of dark pink roses with marjoram, pink larkspur and lavender. If terracotta is used in the finished piece, the pots can be left empty but you could push small, tied bunches of other materials into them or fill them with autumn fruits such as horse chestnuts, fir cones and nuts.

YOU WILL NEED:

Materials:
chicken wire
sphagnum moss
stub (floral) wires
terracotta flowerpots
fabric
mossing (floral) pins
lavender
roses
peonies
dark green moss

Tools:
cutters
pliers
scissors
glue gun

1 Prepare a chicken wire swag approximately 10 cm (4 in) wide, 2.5 cm (1 in) deep and 70–90 cm (2–3 ft) long. Attach terracotta pots at random angles, by passing a stub (floral) wire through the pot and the chicken wire and twisting the two loose ends together with a pair of pliers.

2 Fold a strip of fabric lengthways into three to make a band about 10 cm (4 in) wide. Scrunch up one end of the fabric and pin it to the top of the chicken wire swag, using a mossing (floral) pin or a bent stub wire. Wrap the band of fabric down the length of the frame and around the pots, leaving it to hang fairly loosely. Every 15 cm (6 in) or so, fix the fabric in place with a mossing pin. Make sure that the raw edges of the fabric are always at the back. Once all the fixings are made, go back along the fabric and pull it into its final shape. Scrunch up the other end, tuck it under the last terracotta pot and pin it in place.

3 Make a fabric bow and fix it to the top of the swag with the glue gun. Trim the lavender and roses to a length of 15 cm (6 in) and centre-wire them. Push the stub wire of each bunch into the frame, with a little of the flower covering the fabric. Push each bunch in fairly randomly, criss-crossing the bunches until all the frame and moss is covered. Cut the peony heads from their stems and glue them down the length of the swag. Fill any small spaces with dark green moss.

AUTUMN CANDLE RING

Flat copper rings are harder to find than standard ones, but step 1 shows how to flatten a standard one quite easily. The candle pots are not essential to this design, but when alight, they add magic to the display that is hard to achieve by any other means. Take great care when the candles are lit and never leave them unattended. Many of the materials for this display can be found on a country walk so it is quite inexpensive to make, but preserved leaves look far better and last longer than dried leaves. A good supplier should have a selection of autumn leaves.

YOU WILL NEED:

Materials:
flat or standard
  copper garland ring
florist's dry foam
4 terracotta
  flowerpots
sphagnum moss
reel of florist's wire
preserved oak leaves
stub (floral) wires
twig bundles
eucalyptus seedheads

mushrooms
fir cones
dark green moss
mossing (floral)
  pins
4 candles

Tools:
glue gun
pliers
cutters

1 To make a standard copper ring flat, push or pull the triangular wires towards each other, working all the way round the ring. This will make the ring pull the central circle down, so that the ring becomes flat.

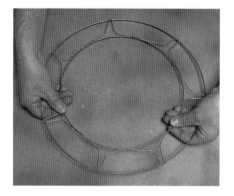

2 Lay the ring on the work surface and flatten it completely with your fingers.

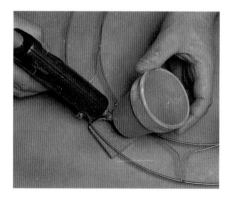

3 Glue a small piece of foam under the ring. Glue a terracotta pot on top, making sure that at least one of the copper wires crosses the centre of the foam. If necessary, change the angle of the copper wire so that it is in the right position. The four pots should be fixed equally round the ring. Continued . . .

4 When the glue has set, cover the ring with sphagnum moss, holding it in place with reel wire. The layer needs to be about 2.5 cm (1 in) thick. Pay particular attention to the base of the ring, making sure that the foam base and the area around the pots is covered.

6 Repeat the process for the bundles of twigs, adding one bundle next to each pot.

5 Make centre-wired bunches of the preserved oak leaves, pushing the stub (floral) wire into the moss base. Make sure that it does not go through the ring but runs along its length. Fill each section between the pots in the same way, using plenty of oak as the main filler.

7 Fix a second bundle in place crossing the first. If the wire is not long enough to hold the bundle firmly in place, use the glue gun to secure it.

8 Add all the other ingredients in the same manner, gluing or wiring them in place and filling all the spaces. Aim to create the feel of a woodland floor. When all of the materials have been added, push dark green moss into place, taking care to fill any small gaps around the edge of the ring. Place a candle in each of the pots and pack them with moss to keep them firmly in place.

VARIATION ON AUTUMN CANDLE RING

Leaf-wrapped candles make a wonderful addition to a dinner table or low cupboard, especially when they are arranged in small groups. Place a little glue on the back of each leaf near the base and press it firmly on to the side of the candle, or use double-sided tape to hold the leaf in place.

Tie a few strands of raffia tightly around the leaves and candle and trim the base of each leaf with scissors, so that the candle stands straight. The leaf used on these candles is preserved magnolia; although quite dark naturally, they have been dyed during the preserving process to produce a very rich burgundy colour.

Avoid using thin candles, as these tend to burn too quickly. The diameter should be at least 8 cm (3 in), with a height of about 15 cm (6 in). Once the flame has reached the level of the top of the leaves, stand the candle on a dish, to ensure that hot liquid wax that spills out through the sides of the leaf does not do any damage. The candle will quite happily burn well down into the centre of the leaves but, for safety's sake, must never be left unattended. When about 2.5 cm (1 in) of candle is left at the bottom, snuff the flame and remove the leaf collar; this will ensure that no accidents occur.

Winter

Although many of the summer grown flowers are now in short supply
a huge range of arrangements can still be created. Spruce is
available now and can be combined with dark roses and Amaranthus
to make beautiful dark rich displays.

EUCALYPTUS TREE

A topiary tree made from preserved eucalyptus stems is well worth the effort it takes to make, because it will last for a very long time. Eucalyptus has a very strong perfume when new which fades a little after a while. Eucalyptus will often arrive in bunches with stems at least 30 cm (12 in) long. They must be trimmed to length, wasting as little material as possible, as close to the leaves as you can; there should be no ugly bare stalks visible in the display. For a fuller, more compact appearance, wire small bunches of eucalyptus and push the stub-wired bunches into the foam between the stems. This will make sure that there are no spaces between stalks.

YOU WILL NEED:

Materials: **Tools:**
terracotta flowerpot   cutters
setting clay   glue gun
length of tree trunk
  about 38 cm
  (15 in) long
florist's dry foam
  sphere about 15 cm
  (6 in) diameter
reindeer moss
mossing (floral) pins
8–10 bunches of
  Eucalyptus spiralus

1 Prepare and make a topiary base. Fix the moss into the top of the terracotta pot all around the base of the tree trunk, using the mossing (floral) pins. Leave the base to dry and harden; allow at least 10 hours. A larger tree in a bigger pot may take about two days to become really hard. If the clay is hard before you add the moss, use the glue gun instead of pins to fix the moss.

2 Cut all the eucalyptus into pieces about 10 cm (4 in) long, trimming the lower leaves so that 2.5 cm (1 in) of stem can be pushed into the foam. Push them, one at a time, into the foam sphere, always keeping hold of the opposite side of the foam, to make sure that you don't push the sphere off the top of the trunk.

3 Keep adding the stems until the whole sphere is covered. Remember to stand back from the display so that you can check that you have added the stems evenly and kept the shape of the sphere.

TIP BOX

Resist the temptation to spray the tree with florist's lacquer; although this will have the desired effect of bringing out the colour of the eucalyptus, it will also destroy the white bloom that covers the leaves.

MARJORAM AND BAY TREE

The ingredients used in this design are mostly herbs. Oregano will keep its colour a very long time, so it's ideal for a brighter location. If you have access to fresh bay stems add them straight from the bush and they will slowly dry out in the display. Although the bulk of the materials here have been added in blocks, a few pieces of each have been mixed with the bulk, to tie the whole design together.

YOU WILL NEED:

Materials:
terracotta flowerpot
setting clay
length of tree trunk
  about 38 cm
  (15 in) long
florist's dry foam
  sphere about 15 cm
  (6 in) diameter
reindeer moss
mossing (floral) pins
8–10 bunches of
  marjoram
stub (floral) wires
bay stems
oregano
twig bundles

Tools:
cutters
glue gun
pliers

1 Prepare and make a topiary base. Fix the moss into the top of the terracotta pot, all around the base of the tree trunk, using the mossing (floral) pins. Leave the base to dry and harden. Allow at least 10 hours.
A much larger tree in a bigger pot may take about two days to become really hard. If the clay is hard when you fix the moss, use the glue gun rather than pins.

TIP BOX

Keep all the bunches as even as possible, and the same length. This helps a great deal when putting the display together, and will ensure that you achieve a perfect sphere. When the display looks a little tired, spray it with florist's clear lacquer. This will bring back some of the colour of the bay and the other materials.

2 Bunch and wire all the marjoram, keeping each bunch to no more than 10 cm (4 in) in length. Push the bunches one at a time into the foam sphere, always holding the opposite side of the foam to which the flowers are being added, to ensure that you don't push the sphere off the top of the trunk. Remember to stand back from the display so that you can check that you have added all the bunches evenly and kept the shape of the sphere.

3 Keep adding the bunches until the whole sphere is covered.

4 Cut the bay stems vertically to separate sprays of one or two leaves. Wire them in bunches or leave them individually. Stub-wire the oregano. Turn the whole display upside-down and push the bay stems and oregano into the foam, all around the base of the trunk. There should be no bay stalks showing. Centre-wire the bunches of twigs and place through the arrangement.

WINTER CONE GARLAND

Take care, when you are bending the larch twigs for this simple garland, that they do not break. Leave some of the small branches longer than you need, so that they stick out from the ring to create interesting angles. Put more material around the bottom of the ring; this will give it a feeling of balance. Take particular care to tuck all the sharp ends of the stub wires back into the display, so that they do not scratch the hanging surface. All the ingredients on this garland will be fairly weather-resistant; even the chillies will take a fair amount of damp winter weather if the ring is hung outside.

YOU WILL NEED:

Materials:	**Tools:**
copper garland ring	cutters
larch cones on twigs	pliers
stub (floral) wires	glue gun
terracotta flowerpots	
chillies	
green moss	
gold spray paint (optional)	
rope or raffia	

1 Cut off the cross wires between the two copper rings and discard them. Cut the wire as close to the ring as possible or, using the pliers, pull the wire away from the ring so that no sharp ends are left. Use either of the rings, depending on the size you want.

2 Tie a larch twig to the ring, using a short piece of stub (floral) wire. Make sure the fixing is as near to one end of the twig as possible. Then, bending the twig gently to the shape of the ring, repeat the fixing on the other end of the twig.

3 Continue with this process until the whole ring is covered with larch twigs and cones. In places where the twigs are small or thin add more than one at a time, crossing the ends of the twigs over each other.

4 Wire two terracotta pots to the ring, by passing a wire through the drainage hole and top of the pot and twisting the loose ends together. This job can be completed before you add all the cones, or at the end.

5 Centre-wire three bunches of chillies and fix these in the same way as the pots. Make sure that the twisted stub-wire ends are pushed back into the display, to hide the sharp ends. Glue small pieces of green moss to the ring to cover the fixings. If you like, frost the garland lightly with gold spray paint. Use rope or raffia to trim with a bow.

WINTER FIREPLACE SWAG

This very grand winter swag uses a dark, rich mixture of materials to create its winter feel. Use the blue pine (spruce) while it is still fresh and it will provide a soft base for the other materials. It will slowly dry out, but it will keep for many months in dry conditions. Use blue pine (spruce) sparingly for a winter swag, rather than a more extravagant Christmas one. Of course, a combination such as this will look good throughout the winter and could be kept in place for the Christmas season, perhaps with additions such as dark red ribbons and gold-sprayed cones. If you hang the swag in the fireplace, keep it away from the open fire.

YOU WILL NEED:

Materials:

rope	dried oranges
red amaranthus	red roses
marjoram	lavender
holly oak	green moss
blue pine (spruce)	mossing (floral)
reel of florist's wire	pins
stub (floral) wires	
cones	**Tools:**
chillies	cutters
kutchi fruit	pliers
	glue gun

1 Cut two lengths of rope to the required length, making a loop at each end for hanging. Trim the waste from the separated bunches of amaranthus, marjoram, holly oak and blue pine (spruce) and make a pile of each material. Using reel wire, tie small bunches of material to the rope base, changing variety with each addition. Work roughly in a zig-zag, making sure that there are no spaces along the bottom edges of the swag. Continue along the whole length of the rope, creating an even mix. Repeat the process for the second rope.

2 Centre-wire and stub-wire the remaining ingredients and place them along the two lengths of swag, roughly where they are required. The cones, oranges and woody items can be glued in place, or wired in the same way as the roses and lavender. Fill any small spaces with moss, pinning or gluing it as you prefer.

TIP BOX

Make the swag in several sections rather than one or two lengths; it is much easier to produce the required shape if each straight length is made separately. Trying to bend the swag into shape will create gaps that are very difficult to hide. When working with a large number of items, it is very easy to forget to add some, so check the work frequently.

QUICK WINTER TABLE CENTREPIECE

Here, two candle pots have been used with a collection of cones and moss to create a very simple winter table-centrepiece. This collection would look just as good on a dark, polished wood surface but take care that the surface is not damaged. Make sure that moss and cones are completely dry before you use them. This design can be made very quickly when time is tight, but will still look quite stunning. Black-watch tartan has been used underneath this display, to create a rich, dark mood.

YOU WILL NEED:

Materials:
florist's dry foam
terracotta flowerpots
candles
mossing (floral) pins
florist's tape
green moss
assorted cones,
  including larch on
  the branch
stub (floral) wires
felt or plastic
  sheeting

Tools:
knife
glue gun
cutters

1 Trim two pieces of foam to produce bases large enough to stand the terracotta pots on. Wire or glue the candles into the pots. Surround the base of the candles, and pots and the sides of the foam with green moss, fixing it in place with mossing (floral) pins.

2 Centre-wire the branches of larch and push the ends of the stub (floral) wire into the foam base. Place one bunch on each side of the four sides of the foam, so that the ends cross each other. Move the arrangement to its final position, putting felt or plastic sheeting underneath. Place all the other ingredients in and around the candles and moss, so that they seem to cascade away from the centre echoing the shape of the table. There are no strict rules for this design, but it should set the mood for the occasion that its made for.

VARIATION ON QUICK WINTER TABLE CENTREPIECE

Exactly the same method has been used to create this variation, with the addition of pomegranates, red chillies, red roses, cinnamon and terracotta flowerpots. The whole display has been placed on a red tartan fabric, and the candle pots have been trimmed with gold cord to create a very special, warm, winter collection. If you need a very large piece, glue several blocks of foam together to create the base. You will need to fix the candle pots in place, and not just stand them on the foam. Push a piece of cane about 7 cm (3 in) long into the foam, leaving about 1 cm (½ in) protruding. Glue around the cane at the base then push the pot on to the cane and leave to set. Use foam and moss to pack the candles tightly in the pots, or glue or wire them.

WOODEN CANDLE BOX

A plain wooden box can be transformed with a small collection of woodland oddments and a candle. This is a place to keep the winter treasures collected while out walking. As there are no fixings except for the candle pot, it is easy to rearrange the ingredients so that the collection looks different all the time. Reflect a whole range of different seasons and environments, from the sea shore, with a box full of pebbles, seashells and starfish, to the depths of winter, with a collection of fruits from the woods. In the height of summer, the lined box can be used to great effect in the centre of a table, overflowing with a range of fresh fruit and several candles.

YOU WILL NEED:

Materials:
florist's dry foam
  block
green moss
mossing (floral) pins
wooden crate or box
terracotta flowerpots
selection of different
  mosses,
  mushrooms, cones,
  nuts and woody
  items, e.g.
  magnolia seedheads
candle
florist's tape

Tools:
knife
glue gun

1 Cut the foam so that it fits into about a third of the box. If the box is open-sided, cover the sides of foam with green moss that will show through the box sides. Fix it in place with mossing (floral) pins or glue.

2 Apply glue to the foam base or to the bottom of the box.

TIP BOX

Changing the colour of the box produces a completely different look, but try to keep to natural colours, such as green or blue, because these look better with natural materials. If you have a large space to fill, especially a deep window sill, a pair of these boxes will do the job very well. Avoid pale-coloured materials, which will fade in the strong light. Don't forget that the candle will need constant attention when burning.

3 Push the block firmly on to the bottom of the box and into the corner. Tease out a little moss through the gaps in the sides of the crate or box. Hold the foam down until the glue has hardened.

4 Cover the remaining sides of the foam with moss, but leave a space on top large enough for the terracotta pot.

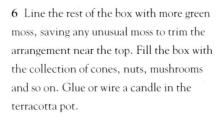

5 Glue the pot firmly to the top of the foam and cover any small spaces with moss.

6 Line the rest of the box with more green moss, saving any unusual moss to trim the arrangement near the top. Fill the box with the collection of cones, nuts, mushrooms and so on. Glue or wire a candle in the terracotta pot.

Christmas

Christmas is a time when we create a large range of arrangements
both as gifts and to decorate our homes. This chapter is filled with
a wide selection of different arrangements to reflect this
rich and festive season.

CHRISTMAS CANDLE POT DISPLAY

This display is designed to make the most of the rich, dark colours of Christmas and to hint at the large variety of edible treats we expect at this special time of the year. To create an even richer look, spray the display with a clear florist's lacquer and lightly frost it with gold paint. Attach a gold fabric bow to the pot with a glue gun and replace the plain church candle with a candle that is heavily perfumed with spices.

YOU WILL NEED:

Materials:

florist's dry foam	kutchi fruit
block	twigs
terracotta flowerpot	chillies
candle	lavender
8 × 13 cm (3 × 5 in)	oranges
candle	cinnamon sticks
mossing (floral) pins	mushrooms
florist's tape	moss
hay	raffia
stub (floral) wires	
red amaranthus	**Tools:**
cones	sharp knife
magnolia leaves	glue gun
holly oak	cutters

1 Trim the foam block to fit snugly into the terracotta pot. Glue or wire the candle to the foam block. Fit the block into the pot. Wire the materials and start to push them into the foam base. Balance is very important. Add the ingredients on alternate sides of the display, starting with the larger items. At this stage, the display ingredients will seem to have a lot of space between them, but you will find that, as the items are added the whole design will begin to take shape.

2 Add all the smaller items, such as the chillies, oranges, cinnamon-stick bundles, lavender, and so on, filling the spaces between the larger items. Trim with the moss, using a glue gun or mossing (floral) pins, so that no foam base shows. The moss can also be used to fill any large gaps between the materials, but be careful not to use too much moss or the general look will be lost. Take particular care to moss around the candle base to cover the fixings.

VARIATION ON CANDLE POT DISPLAY

Although this project looks completely different from the Christmas candle pot, the basic method for construction is nearly the same, without the candle. Instead of filling the basket with a piece of foam, pack a square of chicken wire with moss and form it into a ball shape. Push it into the basket, creating a mound of moss to work on. You can also mix foam offcuts from previous projects with the moss. Start by adding the ingredients at the edge of the basket, centre-wiring or stub-wiring the ingredients as required, and make sure that they hang over the lip, to give the display a well balanced look. Work from one side of the basket to the other, until it is completely covered. Add the chillies and oranges at the end, so that their eye-catching colours do not spoil the balance of the design. Although a fairly exotic collection of items has been used in this display, the basic idea works very well with cones and nuts instead. Once the display has been finished, give it a generous coat of clear florist's lacquer. This will bring out the rich, woody colours and help to prevent the build-up of dust.

For a glitzy, Christmas feeling, the display could be lightly frosted with gold spray paint.

ARTICHOKE CANDLE HOLDER

Choose artichokes that have a fairly flat bottom for this project; it is very important that displays with candles are as safe as possible. These work well as table decorations and you can create a sumptuous setting by giving each place its own candle; candle holders are equally at home in many other locations, however. This candle has been trimmed with gold, to add richness and to match the gold-sprayed base. Other colour combinations work well: white-sprayed artichokes with a white fitted candle, mixed with a collection of dark green moss and white-sprayed pomegranates, make a cool winter centrepiece.

YOU WILL NEED:

Materials:
large globe artichoke
gold spray paint
florist's plastic candle
  holder
dark green moss
short mossing (floral)
  pins
cones
stub (floral) wires
twig bunches and
  cinnamon sticks
  (optional)
candle

Tools:
glue gun
pliers
cutters

1 Spray the artichoke with gold paint. After a few minutes, put some glue in the centre of the artichoke and push the candle holder into the soft glue.

2 Cover the top of the artichoke with moss, fixing it in place with mossing (floral) pins. Make sure the moss covers the sides of the candle holder, but leave the hole at the top clear.

3 Glue or wire in place a carefully balanced selection of cones.

4 You can finish in a variety of ways, with wired bunches of twigs, cinnamon sticks or, as shown here, cones on a twig. Fit the candle in a holder.

BLUE PINE CANDLE POT

When so much blue pine (spruce), combined with roses and cones, is used in a table display, it produces a wonderful Christmas table centrepiece. The blue pine (spruce) is used very fresh, so that its glorious perfume can be enjoyed. As the display dries the perfume will fade, but the pale green needles become slightly darker, which gives the display an even richer appearance.

YOU WILL NEED:

Materials:
florist's dry foam
candle
terracotta flowerpot
florist's tape
mossing (floral) pins
hay
blue pine (spruce)
reindeer moss
cones

stub (floral) wires
roses
kutchi fruit
mushrooms

Tools:
knife
cutters
pliers

1 Fix foam and a candle into a terracotta pot, packing any space with hay. Cut the blue pine (spruce), dividing it into piles from small pieces to large. Starting at the base of the foam, add the largest pieces, pushing them into the foam so that they lean down slightly. Trim the needles from the first 5–8 cm (2–3 in) of the stem, to make it easier to insert the pine (spruce) and to avoid scattering the needles. When adding smaller pieces, use a stub wire to give strength or length.

2 Continue the process, adding more of the larger pieces and working all around the pot. Take the next shorter lengths and add a further layer above the first. Continue until the final and shortest layer is added, nearest to the candle. Remember to keep the pine well away from the base of the candle.

TIP BOX

The terracotta pot used in this display was painted with a dark stain, to match a dark wood table, and the base has felt on it to protect polished surfaces. This mixture works just as well in a dark basket, but make sure that the base is even so that there is no risk of the display toppling over.

Never glue small diameter candles in place, because they need replacing fairly frequently. See the Technique section for how to secure a candle with tape. This makes replacing the candle much faster and easier.

Many other ingredients can be used instead of, or as well as, those shown. Tied bunches of lavender and cinnamon or dried fruit, such as oranges and lemons, also look very good.

3 Fill any large spaces in the display with moss, fixing it in place with mossing (floral) pins. Put plenty of moss around the base of the candle, to cover any fixings. Wire the roses into bunches. Wire the cones, kutchi fruit and mushrooms.

4 Add the wired bunches of roses, the cones and all the other materials, filling in the spaces in the blue pine (spruce).

BLUE PINE TABLE SWAG

The dominant material used in this festive swag is fresh blue pine (spruce). After a few days it will begin to dry out, but it will keep its colour and retain all its needles. Take great care when using the hot glue gun; use it sparingly making sure that it does not run through the display on to the work surface. Any glue that gets on to the display by accident can be covered with the addition of a little moss; simply push it into the hot glue.

YOU WILL NEED:

Materials:
rope
blue pine (spruce)
reel of florist's wire
cones
chillies
stub (floral) wires
mushrooms
pomegranates
reindeer moss
lavender
red roses

Tools:
cutters
glue gun
pliers

1 Cut two lengths of rope; their combined length should be the length you want the swag to be. Cut the blue pine (spruce) about 20 cm (8 in) long. Using the reel wire, bind the stems to the rope.

2 If some of the cones are still attached to stems, bind them to the rope with the reel wire and continue to add the pine (spruce).

3 Continue the process until the whole length of both ropes has been covered. Make sure, as you add the pine (spruce) to the rope, that you don't leave gaps along the edges. Centre-wire the chillies. Fix them along the length of the swag.

4 Glue the mushrooms, loose cones, and pomegranates in place. Then add the reindeer moss.

5 Centre-wire the lavender and roses. Fix them in groups, crossing a bunch of roses with a bunch of lavender. Remember to twist the loose wires under the swag and to tuck the sharp ends back into the bottom of the swag.

To Finish: Where the ends of the swag meet, stand a couple of candles in terracotta pots and surround them with moss. Cover the ends of the swag with the same moss and place a few loose cones and pomegranates on the moss. Protect the table top from the damp moss with a table mat under the display.

CHRISTMAS CHANDELIER

Many different types of ring can be used for this chandelier; the picture shows a ready-made hop-vine garland; its open weave is ideal for fixing things into and on to. More solid cane rings can also be used, but you may need to alter the candle holder so that you can glue it in place. These oranges were dried on a wire rack over the cool end of an Aga and took about four weeks to become completely dry. They can also be dried in a very warm airing cupboard, but this may take a little longer. The oranges are completely dry when the outside skin is very hard and they are much lighter in weight. The ring and the rope have been frosted with a little gold paint and a few starfish have been glued to both, so that the whole chandelier has the same theme.

YOU WILL NEED:

Materials:
dried oranges,
  sprayed gold
gold spray paint
stub (floral) wires
moss
starfish
rope
ready-made hop-vine
  or twig ring
4 florist's candle
  holders
candles

Tools:
knife
small screwdriver
glue gun

1 Cut the oranges in half and make a hole in each half with the screwdriver. Push the two ends of a bent stub (floral) wire through the hole, making a hanging loop. Turn the orange over and bend the ends of the stub wire up, to prevent the loop from falling out.

2 Coat the inside of the orange with glue and push moss into the open space, until you fill it up completely.

3 Place glue on the moss and around the edge of the orange, where the starfish touches it. Hold the starfish in place until the glue sets. Dab a little glue on two or three more starfish and place them on the top and sides of the orange.

4 Bend the top and bottom of a stub wire, hang the decoration on one of the ends and spray it gently with the gold paint. Use the paint so that it provides a frosting rather than a solid colour, letting a little of the orange colour show through.

5 Tie ropes firmly to the ring in four places, so that the chandelier hangs horizontally. The length of rope required will depend on the final hanging position, so at this stage keep the ropes fairly long so you can adjust them afterwards.

6 Push a handful of green moss on to the ring between two ropes. Make a small hole in the centre with your fingers.

7 Put glue in the hole in the moss and push a candle holder into it, making sure that it is completely straight. You may find it helpful to put the candle into the holder to make sure the candle is straight. Hang the oranges on the ring when the ring is in position.

CHRISTMAS TABLE SWAG

You can make one swag for the middle of the table, with all the flowers running in one direction, but it looks far better to make two shorter swags, with the flowers running in opposite directions. The space where the two swags join can then be used for a collection of terracotta pots and candles, to produce a central focal point. The space around the pots and candles here has been filled with tilancia moss and pomegranates, for a warm, sumptuous feeling. For Christmas, a mixture of nuts sprayed gold, with gold glass baubles will give a more glitzy feeling. Place some of the ingredients in and around the swag, so that the additions flow along the length of the table.

YOU WILL NEED:

Materials:
red amaranthus
oregano
red roses
lavender
reel of florist's wire
rope
stub (floral) wires
peonies
cinnamon sticks
green moss
tilancia moss
selection of candles
terracotta flowerpots
pomegranates
raffia

Tools:
cutters
pliers
glue gun

1 Separate all the stems of the various bunches of flowers. Trim them to 15–20 cm (6–8 in), and make a pile of each variety. Using the reel wire, bind the amaranthus and the oregano, in small bunches, down the length of the rope.

2 Continue to cover the rope in this manner, evenly spacing the materials along its entire length. Leave plenty of space between the various bunches, because wired materials will be added later.

TIP BOX

If the table is very long, make the swag in a number of sections; this makes storage of the whole piece far simpler. Wrap the swag in tissue paper and place it in a cardboard box. If the display contains roses and peonies, it is worth spraying the inside of the box with moth repellent. Place the box in a well aired, dry position, such as the loft or in the roof of the garage. Check the box from time to time and re-spray.

3 Stub-wire the roses, lavender and cinnamon sticks. Leave the stub (floral) wire long enough for you to fix the bunches to the swag by pushing the ends through the swag and twisting them together. Push the sharp ends back into the swag, so they do not damage the table surface. Evenly space the tied bunches along the length of the swag.

4 Cut the stems from the peony heads and glue them to the swag, spacing them evenly along its whole length.

Weddings

Although often overlooked for weddings, dried materials
can often produce wonderful effects. Dried flowers,
combined with a matching fabric and a few candles,
will produce a magnificent display.

SUMMER WEDDING TABLE-EDGE SWAG

This is just about the simplest possible swag to make, but used as a table-edge decoration hanging in short loops it gives an impressive finish to the top table or cake table. Conifer is inexpensive to buy and can often be obtained for free from gardens at any time of the year. Pale pink roses are used here for a summer wedding, but you could change the rose colour to give a different feel: red roses mixed with the conifer and used on a dark background would create a wintry look; for spring, pale yellow roses could be used.

YOU WILL NEED:

Materials: **Tools:**
rope   cutters
fresh conifer
reel of florist's wire
pale pink roses

1 Cut the rope to the required length and make a loop at each end. Trim the conifer to short lengths and bind it to the rope, covering it all the way round, with reel wire.

2 Continue this process, adding the pink roses in twos and threes with a handful of conifer stems every few inches. Pack the conifer fairly tightly to produce a thick swag.

TIP BOX

This design isn't long-lasting: the conifer will dry, become brittle and lose its vibrant green colour. If the swags need to be made a few days before the event, hang them in a cool, dry, dark place; this will ensure that the conifer stays looking good and will leave time for other preparations. For a really fresh look, steam the roses to open them up.

SUMMER WEDDING SWAG

This pretty, soft combination is ideal for a summer wedding and can be made any length to fit a particular location. It would look very welcoming placed either side of the church door, or fixed in an arch above it. Making a loop at each end of the rope will ensure that there is a fixing in the right place, to create the right shape. This combination of materials also works well inside the church; made a little larger, it can be wrapped around a stone pillar to make a very impressive effect.

YOU WILL NEED:

Materials: **Tools:**
rope   cutters
nigella   pliers
oregano   glue gun
pink larkspur
reel of florist's wire
stub (floral) wires
lavender
pink roses
gauzy fabric

TIP BOX
Take care to make proper measurements when creating display work for a particular location. Fixing arrangements in place is often quite difficult, because you probably won't be able to drill into the structure of the building. Reel wire and florist's tape will fix most designs in place. If woodwork is to be used for supporting a display, first protect it with the tape and then tie reel wire in place over the tape, to prevent damage. A church will often have permanent fixing positions for the regular display work; make full use of these fixings as they are often quite easy to replace if damaged.

1 Cut the rope to the required length, with a little extra at each end to make the hanging loops. Trim all the waste stems from the materials until they are approximately 15 cm (6 in) in length and make separate piles of each. Start at one end of the rope, tying a small bunch of nigella with the reel wire, to cover the hanging loop.

2 Move along the rope, covering the stems of the nigella with a small bunch of oregano, again fixing it in place with the reel wire. Repeat the process with larkspur.

3 Continue in this order, alternating between the materials and making sure that, when the swag is lying on a flat surface, there are no gaps along its side.

4 Bunch and centre-wire the lavender and roses and add these almost at right angles to the other ingredients. Push the tails of the stub wire through the centre of the swag and twist the ends together, pushing the sharp ends back into the swag. Tie a bow in the fabric and glue it to one end.

WINTER VARIATION ON SUMMER WEDDING SWAG

This winter swag has been made in exactly the same way as the wall-hanging swags shown throughout the book, but it is on a larger scale and has been laid on the floor. A pair of these running either side of the aisle, with a collection of tall candles, makes a stunning display at the front of the church. The moss bow is a chicken-wire frame filled with sphagnum moss, with a thin layer of green moss tied over it with reel wire. Using a swag in this way produces an unusual, eye-catching piece. With matching pew ends it will produce a very complete floral display. Great care needs to be taken with the candles; if the aisle is not very wide it may be wise to do without them.

SUMMER WEDDING CANDLE PILLAR

Candle pillars are fairly easy to make, but only add as much material as you can comfortably hold in one hand, fixing it in place with the reel wire before trying to add more. Experimentation will tell you the best position to hold the candle pillar. You may find it easier to lay the work down while you are adding the materials. Don't add the flowers with too large a gap between each handful of material; gently blend them together. When the display is finished, go back to the top and, if there are any gaps, push a few stems of material between the stems that are already in place.

YOU WILL NEED:

Materials:
small terracotta
  flowerpot
tree trunk
container
setting clay
moss
reel of florist's wire
larkspur
lavender
tall candle
stub (floral) wires or
  mossing (floral) pins

Tools:
cutters
glue gun

1 Using the glue gun, fix the small terracotta pot to the top of the trunk, making sure that it is completely level. Set the trunk in the container.

2 Tuck moss into the base of the pot and wrap it around the trunk, tying it in place with the reel wire. Keep the moss as even as possible and not too thick.

3 Continue the process until the whole trunk has been covered, making sure that the area around the pot at the top of the trunk also has a good layer.

4 Trim the larkspur and lavender to a length of approximately 13 cm (5 in). Starting at the top, tie the larkspur in place using the reel wire.

5 Continue the process, adding the lavender and working down the whole length of the trunk. Each layer should cover the workings of the last. To cover the stem and the wire of the final layer at the base, wrap some green moss around them and fix it in place with mossing (floral) pins. Fix the candle into the small pot with moss or glue.

SUMMER WEDDING PEW END

A collection of these set high on the ends of the church pews produces a dramatic effect, especially if all the candles are burning. These pew ends can be made without the candle, and in a range of different sizes. Start with a small bunch of flowers in an upright position, these will take the place of the canes and the base of the candle. Then add the remaining ingredients in the same criss-cross fashion, to produce a posy shape. If you make a large pew end posy you may find it easier to bind the bunch with reel wire or florist's tape as it grows. Always make sure the stems are fairly long to give a balanced shape to the finished piece.

YOU WILL NEED:

Materials:
two canes 60 cm (24 in) long
40–45 cm (16–18 in) candle
florist's tape
pink larkspur
pink roses
stub (floral) wires
raffia

Tools:
cutters
pliers
scissors

1 Place a cane on either side of the base of the candle. Hold them in place with florist's tape. Make sure the canes are firmly taped in place as tightly as possible.

2 Arrange a layer of flowers around the candle, with the heads just above the height of the tape fixing, holding them in place. Continue the process, adding more and more material and creating a large posy with the candle in the middle.

3 Criss-cross the stems, at an outward angle, to produce a wide, circular display. Tie a stub (floral) wire around the stems and fix it firmly. Tie a raffia bow around the middle to cover the stub wire and attach a strong S-shaped wire at the back to attach the pew end to the fixing on the pew.

TIP BOX
The trick of making a large display from a fairly small amount of material is constantly to criss-cross the stems as the display is built up. When tying the pew ends in their final location, make sure that stub wires hold them firmly in place.

SUMMER POSY

The great advantage of using dried materials for a wedding is that what you are making can be prepared well in advance. Here only two flowers have been used, but any combination can be used to produce a wonderful effect. Make sure that some of the flowers have interest down the stems and not just at the top; the side of the posy is as important as the top surface and is likely to be seen as much. Two bunches of flowers will produce a posy suitable for a young person to carry and four bunches will give you a display nearly twice the size and suitable for someone older. Remember that someone will have to carry the posy and that too much material will make it too large and uncomfortable to hold.

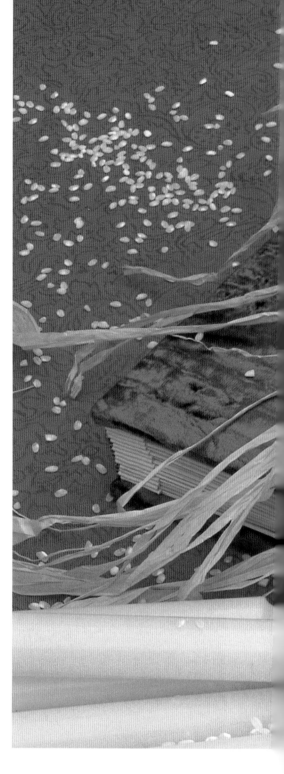

YOU WILL NEED:

Materials: **Tools:**
pink roses   pliers
pink larkspur   cutters
stub (floral) wire
raffia

1 Open and separate the bunches, making two piles of the flowers. Take a mixed handful of flowers in one hand and add more, criss-crossing the materials to produce a small circular display.

2 Wrap a stub (floral) wire around the middle and twist the two ends together, so the posy keeps its shape.

3 Trim away all the waste material, leaving a bunch of short stems just below the stub wire. Make sure this is long enough to hold on to, but still looks neat.

4 Tie the posy with plenty of raffia to cover the stub wire and give a comfortable grip.

WINTER VARIATION ON SUMMER WEDDING PEW END AND SUMMER POSY

Changing the colours gives a completely different feel, even though the designs are the same. Both the pew end and the posy were made previously for a summer wedding, using a selection of pale pinks; here very dark colours have been used for a winter wedding. On the winter posy, the raffia is replaced with a gold and burgundy ribbon that suits the dark mix very well; for the pew end, the raffia was kept but the flowers were wrapped in a dark green fabric to create a rich, heavy feel.

Gifts

Nearly all of the arrangements throughout the book would make a welcome gift, but the elegant pieces on the next few pages use less material than many, and can often be made from leftover pieces. Quick and simple to create they will invariably make delightful, inexpensive presents!

FLOWER-EDGED BASKET

This small, flower-edged basket is similar to the large autumnal flower-edged basket, but the mix of materials is very different and the project has been reduced in size, to make it an ideal gift. A piece of foam has been placed inside the basket, with moss packed around it to keep it in place. The candle sits on top of the foam with no fixing at all. A large-diameter candle like this will stand quite safely, provided that the display is standing on a firm surface, but it should not be left unattended when it is burning.

YOU WILL NEED:

Materials:
rope
stub (floral) wires
reel of florist's wire
sphagnum moss
round basket
Achillea ptarmica
lavender
marjoram
poppy seedheads
mintola balls
green moss
mossing (floral) pins
candle
florist's dry foam
  block

Tools:
knife
glue gun
pliers
cutters

1 Make a sphagnum moss "collar" to fit around the outer edge of the basket. Leaving the poppies and mintola to one side, separate all the flowers and trim them to 15 cm (6 in). Make them into small, centre-wired bunches. Add them, one variety at a time, in small groups, criss-crossing the stems so that some of the flowers face outward and some inward. If the basket is fairly small, you will find that three groups of each material will cover the whole circle with a few spaces to spare.

TIP BOX
Take care with the heavier items when making this design, as they might fall away from the display while the glue is setting. It is worth taking a little extra time to hold them in place until the glue is completely set.

2 Trim the stems from the poppies directly under the seed heads and glue the heads and the mintola balls in small groups around the ring. Use the poppies to cover any stub wires that may be showing on the centre wired bunches of lavender, marjoram and achillea. Be careful to add them in a balanced style.

3 Using the pins, fix green moss in place in any small gaps. Pay particular attention to any stub-wire fixings and the outer edge of the moss collar. Use the moss in generous handfuls so that the collar has an even shape. Put the foam block into the basket and put the candle on top.

DECORATED CLIPFRAME WITH ROSES AND PEONIES

Many displays leave a few leftover bits and pieces; this gift idea is a useful way of using them up. There is no limit to the range of styles that can be created, from heavy, woody looks to soft and pretty arrangements. You may find it easier to fix the photo or picture into the frame before you start. That way you will see if your design will work with a particular picture. Soft-coloured and old pictures tend to work best with natural materials; avoid photographs with very busy backgrounds because this confuses the feel of the frame. For a very soft look, fabric such as lace can be combined with the dried and preserved material; this will look good in a bedroom setting. Picture frames are always welcome gifts, but if your clipframe is to be posted, make sure that it is well packed. A piece of foam in the centre of the picture will help to keep the packaging away from the delicate materials.

YOU WILL NEED:

Materials:
50 × 20 cm
  (10 × 8 in) or
  larger clipframe
preserved or dried
  leaves and ferns
roses
peonies
lavender
epoxy resin glue
raffia

Tools:
scissors
glue gun

1 Make sure that the glass of the clipframe is as clean as possible, removing all finger- and grease marks. Cut the leaves in half, apply epoxy resin glue to the backs and lay the straight edge of each leaf along the straight edge of the frame. Work all the way around the frame, alternating between the top and bottom halves of the cut leaves. Remember that clipframes have fixings that grip the glass edges, so be careful not to get any glue near these clips.

2 Once the epoxy resin has set hard and the leaves are firmly fixed, use the glue gun to stick the ferns in place. Start at one corner and add more on the alternate corner.

3 Steam the roses and peonies open, if necessary. Centre-wire the lavender, and cover the wire with a raffia tie. Glue all the remaining materials in place.

FABRIC-COVERED LAVENDER CANDLE POT

Lavender makes an ideal gift; with its rich colour and long-lasting heady perfume it is always welcome. You could just fill the pot with lavender, leaving the candle out. Adding a few drops of lavender oil will boost the impact of the display and prolong the perfume. Use a fabric that matches the colour scheme of its future surroundings. Trim it with raffia to give a slightly rustic feel or, for a smarter look, trim the pot with a bow made of the same fabric. It's quite possible to use a plastic pot but terracotta makes a safer base for a display incorporating candles. Choose a large candle that will last a long time, so the display need not be disturbed.

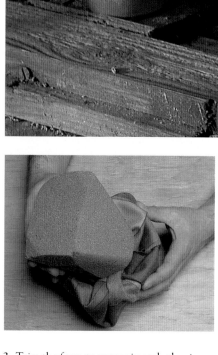

YOU WILL NEED:

Materials:
terracotta flowerpot
fabric
florist's dry foam
candle
mossing (floral) pins
florist's tape
lavender
stub (floral) wires
moss
raffia

Tools:
scissors
knife
glue gun (optional)

1 Put the pot in the middle of the fabric and cut a circle of fabric large enough to wrap up the sides with 8 cm (3 in) to spare.

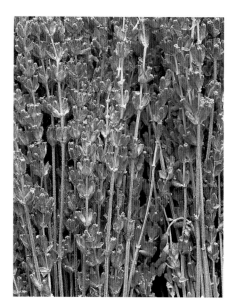

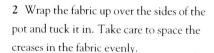

2 Wrap the fabric up over the sides of the pot and tuck it in. Take care to space the creases in the fabric evenly.

3 Trim the foam to approximately the size of the pot making sure it is a tight fit. Push the trimmed foam firmly into the pot right to the bottom, so that it holds the fabric in place.

4 Prepare a candle with mossing (floral) pins or stub wiring and push it into the centre of the foam. Alternatively, glue the candle firmly in place.

5 Wire the lavender into small bunches. Working round the pot, push them into the foam so that they lean well out. Continue this process until you have made a complete circle.

6 Fill the space around the candle with moss. Fix it in place with pins, making sure that it is kept well clear of the candle. Tie a raffia bow around the pot.

CANDLE GIFT-POT

It's important that the wiring for a display of this type is as neat as possible because the foam area is quite small, and untidy wiring runs the risk of splitting the foam. The candle has been pinned and taped in position so that it can easily be replaced.

YOU WILL NEED:

Materials:	Tools:
candle	knife
mossing (floral) pins	scissors
florist's tape	cutters
florist's dry foam	pliers
terracotta flowerpot	
solidago	
Alchemilla mollis	
lavender	
miniature pink roses	
standard pink roses	
pink larkspur	
stub (floral) wires	
green moss	

1 Wire a candle and push it into the foam. Push the foam into the pot, making sure that the foam is about 8 cm (3 in) higher than the rim of the pot. Trim all the ingredients to a length of 10–13 cm (4–5 in), depending on the size of the pot and bunch and wire them. Starting at rim level, push four bunches of solidago into the foam, one on each side of the candle.

2 Repeat this process, adding the flowers in the spaces near the base of the candle. These first two operations will create an S-shaped arrangement of flowers when viewed from the side, running around the display.

3 With the *Alchemilla mollis*, begin to fill the spaces between the solidago; add about eight small bunches. There should be very little space left. Add eight bunches of lavender, again in an S-shape. If there are any large spaces at this point fill them with solidago or *Alchemilla mollis*.

4 Randomly add the small bunches of miniature and standard roses, filling all the small gaps. If you have used all the roses, add another material. In this display, larkspur was included because the rose-bunches were a little smaller than needed.

5 Trim the base of the candle and the rim of the pot with green moss, using the mossing (floral) pins to hold it in place.

VALENTINE POT POURRI

This is a wonderful way of making use of spare flower pieces from other displays. The plain cardboard box used for this mixture has been covered with a broad red ribbon and a piece of the same ribbon has been cut in half to create the decoration on the top of the box. Essential oil will discolour the materials in the box over a period of time. This can be avoided by letting the drops fall only on to the moss; with the lid closed the perfume will still be imparted to the flowers. This is not so long-lasting as pot pourri made the traditional way, but it's a quick and quite effective method when time is short.

YOU WILL NEED:

Materials: **Tools:**
box   cutters
red and pink   scissors
  rosebuds, or any
  suitable assortment
lavender
reindeer moss
rose or lavender
  essential oil

1 Line the bottom of the box with rose leaves and a few stems of lavender. Trim the stems of the lavender fairly short, using mostly the flower heads.

2 Place some of the reindeer moss in the box, around the flower heads.

3 Trim the heads from the stems of all the remaining flowers and arrange them in the box. Add a few fresh flower heads if you wish, but make sure they are not too woody otherwise they won't dry out.

4 Gently drizzle a few drops of the essential oil over the reindeer moss, to give the flowers a gentle perfume.

TOOLS AND EQUIPMENT

Canes: These can be used for extending the length of stems, when creating a large display. They are useful for any number of other jobs, including building a frame for a square or triangular garland and helping to fix terracotta pots in a display.

Clear florist's spray or lacquer: Used with care, this will enhance the colour of many materials and help to hold delicate petals in place. It's also good for sealing a surface to help prevent the absorption of moisture.

Copper garland rings: In a variety of sizes, these are used as the base for garlands. Ideal if the design has large or heavy elements.

Cutters: Choose a good, strong pair of sprung cutters – small secateurs (pruning shears) – that suit your hand. Florists tend to use strong scissors and you may find these quite adequate. Cutters with a spring make light work of most materials.

Fire-retardant spray: This is especially useful for displays using candles or that will be used near fireplaces.

Florist's adhesive tape: Good for binding blocks of oasis together or for holding the oasis in place in a basket.

Florist's dry foam blocks, pyramids and spheres: These are usually grey in colour and are now available as an environmentally-friendly product. Make sure that you do not buy the kind of florist's foam (oasis) intended for fresh flowers: this will crumble if it's used with dried flowers.

Florist's plastic candle holders: These are available in various sizes. Simply push them into a florist's dry foam block.

Glue gun: One of the most useful tools, it's really worth buying one of these, rather than struggling with tubes of glue. Do not buy the cheapest that you can find as these tend to be rather hard to use. Make sure that the gun you buy has a trigger feed for the glue as this makes life a lot easier. A hot glue gun is much to be preferred, because the glue sets much more quickly.

Hessian (burlap): Used to protect the surface against which swags and garlands are hanging, hessian can also be used as a smart, effective trim. Fix it with mossing pins, or sew it in place with a strong thread.

Knives: Choose two sharp knives, one short and one long. These will mostly be used for cutting foam and it helps if you use a sharp knife. This will prevent the foam from crumbling.

Mossing (floral) pins: These are ready-made horseshoe-shaped pins or they can easily be made from stub wires cut to the required length. Used mainly for fixing moss into place, they are also very useful for many other jobs where a small fixing is needed.

Pliers: For securing and twisting stub (floral) wires and general heavy-duty jobs.

Reel (spool) wire: This comes in a range of different gauges and is ideal for swags and garlands. Choose a gauge that is not too heavy.

Scissors: These need to be sharp for trimming fabric, etc. Resist using them for cutting stems, which will quickly blunt them.

Setting clay: For filling the bottom of baskets to weight them down so they don't topple, and to set trunks into for topiary trees.

Staple gun: A useful tool, especially for fixing chicken wire frames to woodwork. Choose a model that can easily be taken apart: they are prone to jamming.

String: Choose a good-quality, strong string; gardener's string is often the best and tends to be of a colour to suit the work.

Stub (floral) wires: These are available in a number of different lengths and gauges. The long wires are the best value because they can easily be cut down to shorter lengths. Do not be tempted to buy too thin a gauge as they will not hold woody stems in place.

Use the tools and equipment specified in the project whenever you can. It makes the work much easier.

MATERIALS

When selecting your materials, choose carefully. If they are shop-bought, make sure the stock is bright in colour and not too brittle. If the shop you go to has a dull, boring collection it is probably old and should be avoided. Check the flowers for moth damage, especially roses and peonies because they are particularly prone to attack. Look inside the flowers and don't buy any with grubs or eggs in. All dried flowers will lose some material when handling, but avoid any that drop a lot of petals; they will have been stored badly. Items such as branches, twigs and moss can be used fresh, in fact they are much easier to work with when a little damp. Displays using these items must be left in a warm dry place when completed so that they can completely dry out.

It is well worth mastering the skill of drying your own flowers and materials. Air-drying is the easiest and most successful method. You will need a place with a constant flow of warm, dry air, such as an airing cupboard or a space above an Aga. Dry woody items on a wire rack; they may take some time. Flowers can be tied and hung upside-down and will take much less time. If the drying space is light, cover or wrap the materials with newspaper, making sure that air can still circulate around them. Experiment: even daffodils can be dried, producing wonderful results.

If shop-bought flowers have dried out a little too much, hang them in a moist room such as the kitchen or bathroom for a day or two; this will let them absorb some moisture and make them much easier to work with. Don't leave them longer or the material may become too damp and start to rot. If they feel too soft after a couple of days, reverse the process by placing them in a dry, warm airing cupboard.

Achillea filiendulina This mustardy yellow plant has been a favourite for many years. The large head fills spaces quickly and seems to be a necessity for any large, country-style arrangement. Easy to keep dust-free, the heads can be dusted with a soft brush and a hair dryer.

Achillea ptarmica Clusters of small, bright white flowers on dark green stems. Use with care; this bright white tends to stand out when combined with other materials. They have a very long life but need to be kept away from damp, or the white will turn to pale brown very quickly.

Alchemilla mollis A beautiful material to use, and one that can be added to all types of display, giving a soft feel. The colour will fade to a soft yellowy brown. It tends to break quite easily. Very easy to grow, it can be found in most English country gardens.

Amaranthus (Love-lies-bleeding) Most commonly seen either in natural dark green or dyed dark red. The variety shown here is long and upright, but it is also available as a long, soft tail. Be selective when choosing bunches; their thickness and length vary tremendously. For small display work, use the thinner variety. *Amaranthus caudatus* is particularly attractive for dried-flower arrangements; its pretty pale green colour makes it very appealing in spring displays.

Ambrosinia Widely available in two versions, one short and one long, this pale green plant has a wonderful scent that is especially strong when it is being worked with. As with all green material, avoid strong light so that the colour is maintained. In a centrally heated house it will dry out and become very fragile, so put it in a traffic-free location, if possible.

Anaphalis margaritacea A fluffy white flower that is extremely easy to grow. The flowers dry in the garden on the stem. Make sure you pick them before they start to go to seed, or you will have a room full of fluff. The greeny yellow centre makes a good match with other materials and the pale white of the flower is easy to live with.

Bupleurum griffiti This green plant is a useful filler. Care needs to be taken when using it in light conditions, because the green will fade fast. Each stem has a large number of heads, each with a collection of small seeds. Each small head is ideal as a filler between other flowers, when making small display pieces.

Chinese lanterns (physalis) This paper-thin orange form is another well used material, but it still deserves a place on the flower arranger's list. The vivid orange colour will not last if exposed to strong light. It is a fairly easy plant to grow in the garden, although you will probably not have as many seed pods on the home-grown varieties as on those grown commercially.

Cobra leaves Large, preserved leaves, very useful for wrapping and coating containers.

Copper beech (*Fagus sylvatica*) This dark brown leaf is an extremely good backdrop, combined with any number of dried materials. It can be used in its natural condition collected from the woods, although the leaves tend to curl as it dries out. It is best used as a preserved material; it will then keep for an indefinite period.

Echinops ritro 'Veitch's Blue' When they are at their best, the globe-shaped heads are a deep steely blue. Handle with some care: they are prone to break apart. Always look for the new season's stock because they handle much better when they are fresh. Echinops are quite expensive to buy but very easy to grow in the right conditions.

Echinops sphaerocephalus The same family as the blue echinops but a much larger variety with silvery-blue heads. They take spray colour very well and are very useful for Christmas decorations or for displays that need drama. Handle with care, because the flower heads are very spiky.

Eucalyptus spiralus Available mostly as a preserved product, this wonderful leaf normally comes in two colours, green and brown. A joy to work with, because it gives off a beautiful scent when the stems and leaves are bruised. The scent will last for months and will often be noticed long before the display is seen. Eucalyptus is ideal for large displays that require long stems.

Globe artichoke If you can bear not to eat these wonderful plants, they are well worth drying. They make a huge statement, either in full bloom or when they are quite small, and they deserve to be displayed alone, standing in a large vase. The outside comes in a range of green and purple colours; when they are in full bloom the centre is a mass of delicate mauve fronds. To dry them, hang them upside-down, wrapped in paper with the bottom open over a constant flow of warmth. They will take two or three weeks to dry.

Golden mushrooms These mushrooms can give a remarkable lift to all types of display. They will frequently be found with ready-fixed stems, so they can easily be added to a display. If yours have no stems you will need to add them. This is best done with a glue gun. They also welcome a light spray of clear florist's lacquer, to bring out the rich, dark, woody colours.

Holly oak (*Banksia serrata*) This very large leaf is usually preserved. It makes a good substitute for holly and, because it is pre-served, will not lose its shape or dry out. Spray it with paint to make a perfect colour match or gild it lightly with gold for a winter decoration. It is also a good filler for a large display.

Hydrangea macrophylla These are one of the most useful dried materials, which come in a range of colours from very dark pink through to a pale almost-grey and a variety of tones to dark blue. They can be dried very easily at home, in a constantly light-free, warm area. The large heads very quickly fill a display and they have a very long life.

Immortelle (xeranthemum) Small, star-shaped mostly purple or white flowers, they have an extremely long shelf life and tolerate bright light very well. Often used as a filler because they are rather inexpensive, they need to be used with care because the strong purple colour will dominate a display.

Kutchi fruit A caramel-coloured seed pod with a vanilla aroma.

Larkspur (consolida) Very close to the delphinium, these flowers come in a range of colours but are most commonly blue, pink or white. Faded colours usually mean that the stock has been around for a while. If the bunches are a little crushed, revive them with a very gentle steaming. Probably one of the most useful display flowers.

Dutch lavender (Lavandula) This is a paler-coloured lavender, with more uniform stems and a stronger scent.

French lavender *Lavandula stoechas* This variety is a magnificent blue and should be used in just about all displays: its rich colour is outstanding. Take care when buying it, because the quality often varies.

Marjoram Another very useful herb. The dark purple and green works well with most

materials, especially roses, peonies, nigella and lavender.

Mintola balls These woody seedpods are similar in appearance to small coconuts. They are often supplied with wooden stakes attached; these can be trimmed off if not required.

Mosses The main types of moss used in this book are sphagnum moss, tilancia moss, green wood moss, lichen moss and reindeer moss. Although all can be purchased dried, only tilancia moss is really suitable for use in this condition; the other varieties are best used slightly damp and then left to dry out completely in the display.

Nicandra (physocarpus) This green seed pod is a nice, smaller alternative to the orange Chinese lantern. The pale colour can be used with many other colours and the shape gives a distinctive texture to an arrangement. Green does *not* like bright light, so keep this away from direct sunlight. In time, the green will turn dark brown, but for a seed pot this is quite acceptable.

Nigella damascena) (Love-in-a-Mist) A real favourite, these seed pods combine purple and green colours with an unusual shape. However, they dislike bright light and will fade very fast. A good material for special-occasion displays, in which the colour can be enhanced or changed with the use of spray paints, for example, spray it gold or silver for Christmas.

Nigella orientalis This is the same family as Love-in-a-Mist, but a completely different shape. All green, it is susceptible to loss of colour but the very unusual shape more than makes up for this. Usually it has quite a short season, so it's not always available.

Oak (quercus) This is a leaf used in a similar way to preserved copper beech. The leaf

tends to be a little thicker and will stand the test of time even better. In its preserved state it will often have a little brown dye added. This helps to give the leaf a dark, rich colour that will last.

Oregano This well-loved herb makes a lovely dried plant that can be used over and over again. It has a very unusual texture and releases a beautiful scent. The colour will keep indefinitely; it is certainly one of the more robust plants. Any unused pieces can be kept to form part of a pot pourri; they mix well with lavender and rose petals.

Peony (paeonia) These have a very short season but are well worth hunting for. Although a little expensive to buy, they are quite easy to dry at home, if you are careful. Mostly dark pink, they can also be a rich pinky cream. A note of caution: moths have a love affair with peonies. Do make sure that there are no eggs in the flower before you bring them indoors, because these moths also like fabrics.

Poppy seedhead (papaver) Although these seed pods are very common, they are worth considering for any display. Ranging from a dark powder-grey through to greeny-grey, they will suit most colour schemes. Avoid spraying them with florist's clear lacquer, which will destroy the powdery bloom that is such an attractive feature of the seed pod. Do not use the seeds from the pod on food.

Protea compacta (Cape honey flower) This woody head will last for ever and needs only a light dusting to maintain its good looks. A range of different sizes is available. You will need a strong pair of cutters to cut the stems.

Rat's-tail statice (*Limonium suworwii* or *Psylliostachys suworwii*) These dark to pale pink flowers come in a huge variety of lengths. Although they will mostly be fairly straight when fresh, they tend to drop after a time.

They look their best used in small bunches rather than as single stems and they add a very distinct texture to the finished display.

Rosa paleander These are the miniature version of the standard dried rose and not generally prone to moth attack. They are available in a huge range of colours. Watch out for the thorns, which are particularly vicious on these small roses. They look particularly good combined with the larger roses.

Roses A wide range of different colours is available. One of the most expensive of all dried flowers, they are also the most exquisite. Always save them until last so that the rose heads do not get broken while you are constructing the display. Most varieties will welcome a little steaming, to ease the shape and increase the size. This releases a beautiful scent and is a sheer joy to perform. They are prone to attack from moths and need to be inspected for eggs from time to time. If you find any, discard the flowers at once; these moths like fabric.

Safflower (carthamus) Two main varieties are available, with and without flowers. The dark ginger flower is often used to make dye. They make a stunning addition to a display. The bunches tend to be fairly large and need to be split and wired. Choose only the flowers which have deep green leaves and dark orange flowers. This indicates that the stock is fresh.

Sanfordii These small clusters of bright yellow flowers make a striking addition to a display. The golden yellow colour has a very long life, although the flower heads do need to be supported by other materials or the weight of the flowers will bend the stems. This looks very ugly and will spoil the arrangement.

Apart from the wonderful selection of dried and preserved flowers available, there is also an enormous number of other materials. Here is a small selection of some of the alternatives. Some of them, such as the pomegranates, apples, mushrooms and chillies, can very easily be dried at home in a dark, dry, warm place. The pomegranates will take a number of weeks to dry and the thin, papery mushrooms can be dry in a few hours. The simple rule is to check every day; when the product is lighter in weight and hard to touch, all the moisture will have evaporated.

Sea holly (eryngium) Clusters of small blue thistles, this is a plant to be handled with the gloves on! It's very spiky but worth the effort. Sea holly has a long life, with the blue colour lasting a long time. As it fades it becomes grey/green turning to a pale brown. *Eryngium alpinum* is an attractive species with purplish-blue, cone-shaped flower heads, and a frilly "collar".

Silene (campian) This tiny pink flower looks as though it is fresh, even when dried. It will lose some petals as you work with it, but not enough to matter. The colour keeps for a long time and you only need to add this flower in small quantities. The small flower heads create a soft look in the finished display. Give the flowerheads some support, to stop them hanging down.

Solidaster A hybrid species made by crossing solidago and aster, this is a pale yellow flower that keeps its colour well. Bunches are fairly large and will go a long way. Each stem has dozens of flowers that can be wired into small bunches. It makes a good filler, if the pale yellow colour suits your needs.

Strawflower (helichrysum) This has to be one of the best known dried flowers and has slipped from favour with many arrangers. However it still has a place: the range of colours is vast and the flower head has a very long life. Used in bunches rather than as single flowers, it can look quite stunning.

Sunflower (helianthus) These large yellow flowers are well known but have only recently been added to the list of dried materials. The yellow petals tend to be quite small and

also have a tendency to fade, but sunflowers are a very good flower for large extravagant displays. The stems can easily be extended simply by pushing a cane up into the hollow of the stem.

Tolbos (top brush) A spiky form of protea that is becoming more widely available. It has a furry centre and usually bears a number of heads on each stem.

Wheat Wheat is only one of a number of grasses available. Although grasses are very attractive, they need to be used with care. Their green colour has a very short life, and no other range of dried material has given dried display work a worse reputation. Until recently, many people could only see dried flowers as brown and boring and this image was largely due to grasses.

SUPPLIERS

There are numerous stockists of dried materials, but the following are recommended as being particularly reliable suppliers of good quality dried flowers. In time, you may find that a supplier changes direction and does not stock the range that you require. All the materials you need to make the designs in this book can be obtained from Terence Moore Designs, which also undertakes special commissions and runs one-day workshops for individuals and groups.

When buying dried stock, make sure that it is as fresh as possible and has plenty of colour. If the material looks muddy or is brittle to touch, then it has been in stock for longer than is desirable and should be avoided. Suppliers who stock only a small range of dried materials will probably have a slow turnover, so you should avoid buying from them.

UNITED KINGDOM

Terence Moore Designs
The Barn Workshop, Burleigh Lane
Crawley Down, West Sussex RH10 4LF
Tel./Fax: (01342) 717944

The Bay Tree Florist
19 Upper High Street, Thame
Oxon OX9 3EX
Tel: (01844) 217993

Bright Ideas
38 High Street, Lewes
East Sussex BN7 2LU
Tel: (01273) 474395

Country Style
358 Fulwood Road, Ranmoor
Sheffield S10 3GD
Tel: (01742) 309067

De La Mares Florist
Rue A Don, Grouville, Jersey
Channel Islands
Tel: (01534) 851538

Forsyths
7 Market Place, St Albans
Herts AL3 5DK
Tel: (01727) 839702

Hilliers Garden Centre
London Road (A30), Windlesham
Surrey GU20 6LN
Tel: (01344) 23166

Hilliers Garden Centre
Woodhouse Lane, Botley
Southampton SO3 2EZ
Tel: (01489) 782306

Lesley Hart Dried Flowers
37 Smith Street, Warwick CV34 4JA
Tel: (01926) 490356

Mews Gallery
Old Stone House, 23 Killenchy Comber
Co. Down, Northern Ireland BT23 5AP
Tel: (01247) 874044

Page and Bolland
Denscombe Mill, Shillingford, Tiverton
Devon EX16 9BH
Tel: (01398) 6283

Three French Hens
Home Farm, Swinfern, Nr Lichfield
Staffs WS14 9QR
Tel: (01543) 481613

UNITED STATES

American Oaks Preserving Company, Inc.
601 Mulberry Street, North Judson
Indiana, 46366
Tel: (800) 348-5008; Call for local retailers.

Earthstar Herb Gardens
438 West Perkinsville Road
China Valley, Arizona, 86323
Tel: (602) 636 2565; Catalog $1.00.

Fischer & Page, Ltd.
134 West 28th Street, New York
NY 10001 (wholesale).

Gold Mine Catalog
W10635, Highway 1, Reeseville
Wisconsin, 53579
Tel: (414) 927-3603; Catalog $2.00.

Herb Gathering
5742 Kenwood, Kansas City
Missouri, 64110
Tel: (816) 523-2653; Catalog $2.00
(refundable)

J&T Imports
P.O. Box 642, Solana Beach
California, 92075 (wholesale)

LeeWards
Main Ofice, Elgin, Illinois, 60120
Tel: (708) 888-5800; Call for local retailers.

Meadow Everlasting
R.R. 1, 149 Shabbona Road, Malta
Illinois, 60150
Tel: (815) 825-2539; Catalog $1.00.

Patchogue Florals Fantasyland
10 Robinson Avenue, East Patchogue
New York, 11772
Tel: (516) 475-2059.

Stamens & Pistils
875 Third Avenue, New York, NY 10022
Tel: (212) 593-1888

Sun Kempt
P.O. Box 231, Yorkviller, NY 13495
Tel: (315) 797-9618; Catalog $1.00
(refundable).

Tom Thumb Workshop
Rt. 13, Box 357, Mappsville
Virginia, 23407
Tel: (804) 824-3507; Catalog $1.00.

Wayside Gardens
1 Garden Lane, Hodges, South Carolina
29695-0001
Tel: (800) 845-1124; Free catalog.

Well-Sweep Herb Farm
317 Mount Bethel Road, Port Murray
New Jersey, 07865
Tel: (201) 852-5390; Catalog $1.00.

CANADA

Crafts Canada
440-28 Street, NE, Calgary
Alberta T2A 6T3
Tel: (403) 569-2355

Multi-Crafts and Gifts
2210 Thurston Drive, Ottawa
Ontario, K1G 5L5

Index

ACKNOWLEDGEMENTS

A project of this nature is always a team effort. I would like to thank
all those involved for their hard work, but special thanks go to the following:
Suzy, my wife, who always gets the short straw and ends up supplying tea and
coffee and doing all the running around; Michelle Garrett and Dulci, for producing
such wonderful pictures; Joanne Rippin, who has shown great patience;
Helen Sudell and Joanna Lorenz, for giving their time and support.
And thanks are also due to the following friends, who have been in the background
and often giving far more than just a helping hand: John and Veronica Sutton;
Ian and Andrea; John Warner; Jenny and Tony. Finally, a very special thanks
and much love go to my two sons Nicholas and William, who, on the whole,
left me alone to write and frequently ended up with some of my domestic jobs.